AMERICAN
WAR LIBRARY
★ ★ ★ ★

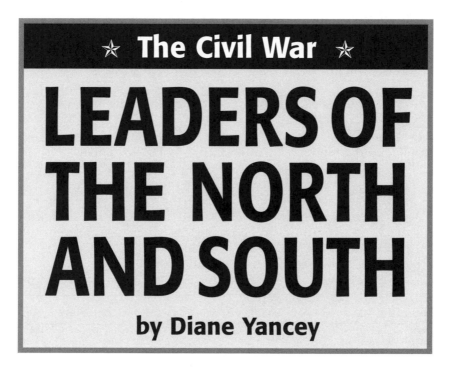

★ The Civil War ★

LEADERS OF THE NORTH AND SOUTH

by Diane Yancey

Lucent Books, P.O. Box 289011, San Diego, CA 92198-9011

Titles in The American War Library series include:

World War II
Hitler and the Nazis
Kamikazes
Leaders and Generals
Life as a POW
Life of an American Soldier in
  Europe
Strategic Battles in Europe
Strategic Battles in the Pacific
The War at Home
Weapons of War

The Civil War
Leaders of the North and South
Life Among the Soldiers and
  Cavalry
Lincoln and the Abolition of
  Slavery
Strategic Battles
Weapons of War

Library of Congress Cataloging-in-Publication Data

Yancey, Diane.
    Leaders of the North and South / by Diane Yancey.
        p.   cm.—(American war library. The Civil War)
    Includes bibliographical references and index.
    Summary: Discusses the leaders of the Civil War and their
accomplishments, including statesmen, abolitionists, commanders
of the Union and the Confederacy, cavalrymen, and women
of courage.
    ISBN 1-56006-497-8 (lib. bdg. : alk. paper)
    1. United States—History—Civil War, 1861–1865—Biography—
Juvenile literature. 2. Leadership—History—19th century—
Juvenile literature. [1. United States—History—Civil War,
1861–1865—Biography.] I. Title. II. American war library. Civil War.
E467.Y37   2000
973.7'092'0—dc21   99-046314
                                                                              CIP

Copyright 2000 by Lucent Books, Inc.
P.O. Box 289011, San Diego, California 92198-9011

Printed in the U.S.A.

★ Contents ★

A Nation Forged by War

The United States, like many nations, was forged and defined by war. Despite Benjamin Franklin's opinion that "There never was a good war or a bad peace," the United States owes its very existence to the War of Independence, one to which Franklin wholeheartedly subscribed. The country forged by war in 1776 was tempered and made stronger by the Civil War in the 1860s.

The Texas Revolution, the Mexican-American War, and the Spanish-American War expanded the country's borders and gave it overseas possessions. These wars made the United States a world power, but this status came with a price, as the nation became a key but reluctant player in both World War I and World War II.

Each successive war further defined the country's role on the world stage. Following World War II, U.S. foreign policy redefined itself to focus on the role of defender, not only of the freedom of its own citizens, but also of the freedom of peo-

ple everywhere. During the cold war that followed World War II until the collapse of the Soviet Union, defending the world meant fighting communism. This goal, manifested in the Korean and Vietnam conflicts, proved elusive, and soured the American public on its achievability. As the United States emerged as the world's sole superpower, American foreign policy has been guided less by national interest and more on protecting international human rights. But as involvement in Somalia and Kosovo prove, this goal has been equally elusive.

As a result, the country's view of itself changed. Bolstered by victories in World Wars I and II, Americans first relished the role of protector. But, as war followed war in a seemingly endless procession, Americans began to doubt their leaders, their motives, and themselves. The Vietnam War especially caused people to question the validity of sending its young people to die in places where they were not particularly wanted and for people who did not seem especially grateful.

While the most obvious changes brought about by America's wars have been geopolitical in nature, many other aspects of society have been touched. War often does not bring about change directly, but acts instead like the catalyst in a chemical reaction, accelerating changes already in progress.

Some of these changes have been societal. The role of women in the United States had been slowly changing, but World War II put thousands into the workforce and into uniform. They might have gone back to being housewives after the war, but equality, once experienced, would not be forgotten.

Likewise, wars have accelerated technological change. The necessity for faster airplanes and a more destructive bomb led to the development of jet planes and nuclear energy. Artificial fibers developed for parachutes in the 1940s were used in the clothing of the 1950s.

Lucent Books' American War Library covers key wars in the development of the nation. Each war is covered in several volumes, to allow for more detail, context, and to provide volumes on often neglected subjects, such as the kamikazes of World War II, or weapons used in the Civil War. As with all Lucent Books, notes, annotated bibliographies, and appendixes such as glossaries give students a launching point for further research. In addition, sidebars and archival photographs enhance the text. Together, each volume in The American War Library will aid students in understanding how America's wars have shaped and changed its politics, economics, and society.

A National Perspective

Pulitzer Prize–winning author Robert Penn Warren once wrote, "The Civil War is, for the American imagination, the great single event of our history."[1] The leaders of that war were equally exceptional and unique. They drafted policies, roused public passions, battled and led others into battle, and guided the nation through four years of turmoil unlike anything it had ever experienced before.

They were as varied as America itself: gentleman and slave, Union man and secessionist, abolitionist and slaveholder. They came from different backgrounds and shouldered their responsibilities in different ways. Some were flamboyant and outgoing, others modest and retiring. Some came out of the war with glowing reputations; others were controversial because of their actions. Yet all were patriots. All defined what they thought was important to do and did it. All played a part in an upheaval that shook the very foundations of the United States of America.

Unbridgeable Divisions

Few Americans in the mid-1800s foresaw war as the inevitable outcome of America's long-standing economic, political, and emotional differences. After eighty years of nationhood, however, divisions between North and South were deep and unbridgeable. Southerners based their economy on crops such as tobacco and cotton, tended by millions of slaves on whom they relied to maintain their gracious, unhurried way of life. They placed strong emphasis on states' rights—the idea that states, not the federal government, have the right to decide most issues that affect their citizenry.

Northerners, on the other hand, emphasized industry, education, and hard work; valued liberty as much as patriotism; and had repudiated slavery, which denied men, women, and children their freedom. Northerners held that the federal government took precedence over state governments and that federal leaders had the right to legislate whether certain practices were right or wrong, moral or immoral. Over the years, the issue of slavery alone had become an axis around which bitter and unanswerable national arguments seemed to endlessly revolve.

The Last Straw

Abraham Lincoln's election as president of the United States in November 1860 was the last straw for Southerners, who rightly believed that the new president was morally opposed to slavery. They mistakenly believed that he would abolish it upon taking office, however. Lincoln tried to soothe their fears, saying in his first inaugural address, "I have no purpose, directly or indirectly, to interfere with the institution of slavery in the states where it exists. I believe I have no lawful right to do so, and I have no inclination to do so."[2]

Sleeping Serpent

Early leaders of the United States had not been able to agree on the issue of slavery, and thus they pushed the argument aside for later generations to deal with. Nevertheless, the topic continued to be a controversial one, as Geoffrey C. Ward points out in *The Civil War: An Illustrated History.*

Most Americans spoke the same language, tilled the same soil, worshiped the same Protestant God. They also shared a common pride in first having wrested independence from the mightiest power on earth, Great Britain, and then for having carved an energetic, fast-growing country out of a wilderness. Above all, they were boastful about the republican institutions they had devised and with which they had governed themselves for seventy-one years, institutions which, nearly all Americans agreed, were the envy of every other people on earth.

But from the first there was one issue that more than any other divided North from South. "There was never a moment," during the earliest years of our national history, wrote the essayist John Jay Chapman, "when the slavery issue was not a sleeping serpent. That issue lay coiled up under the table during the deliberations of the Constitutional Convention in 1787. It was owing to the cotton gin, more than half awake at the time of the Louisiana Purchase in 1803. . . . Thereafter slavery was on everyone's mind, though not always on his tongue."

Two slaves operate a cotton gin. The South's economy depended on cotton and the labor of slaves to pick and process it.

Southerners refused to believe his assertions. Unrest grew, emotions heightened, and on December 20, 1860, South Carolina became the first state to secede (break away) from the Union. Five others—Mississippi, Florida, Alabama, Georgia, and Louisiana—followed suit in January. By spring, those six, plus Texas, Virginia, Arkansas, North Carolina, and Tennessee, formed the Confederate States of America, with Jefferson Davis elected as first president.

The Nation Goes to War

The nation had split apart, and war was in the air. Rational men like Lincoln continued to hope and believe that peaceful means could be found to solve the country's difficulties. Others became convinced that physical force was the inevitable answer to the controversy. Radical abolitionist John Brown wrote before he was hanged in 1859, "I John Brown am now quite certain that the crimes of this guilty land; will never be purged away; but with blood."[3]

As Brown anticipated, war broke out on April 12, 1861, when Confederates shelled Fort Sumter, a Federal garrison located in Charleston Harbor, South Carolina. Sumter fell a day later; both sides put out a call for troops; and within two months the war was in full swing. The North's initial objective was the preservation of the Union in its entirety, but as time passed the issue of slavery became paramount and all but eclipsed the pri-

mary aim. "We were no longer merely the soldiers of a political controversy," wrote one soldier. "[We] were now the missionaries of a great work of redemption, the armed liberators of millions. . . . The war was ennobled; the object was higher."[4]

Early in the conflict, Confederate enthusiasm, their willingness to defend their soil against Yankee (Northern) invaders, and the genius of Confederate commanders such as Robert E. Lee, Thomas "Stonewall" Jackson, and J. E. B. Stuart more than counterbalanced the North's large reserves of men, money, and matériel. As time passed, however, Lincoln's blockade of Southern ports cut off vital European imports that the South needed in order to fight. A lack of cooperation among Confederate leaders undermined Rebel (Southern) fighting spirit. Hundreds of battles, clashes, skirmishes, and free-for-alls taught Union commanders like Ulysses Grant, William Sherman, and Philip Sheridan how to fight and win. Southern strength gradually eroded until, by April 1865, not even the most loyal Confederate could justify a continuation of the fight.

God's Purposes

Most Americans—leaders and common people alike—came out of the war unprepared for the changes the mighty conflict had produced. The Union had been saved and slavery abolished. Tremendous physical, social, and emotional devastation had occurred, which needed to be addressed before the country could heal.

Ironies of War

The Civil War remains one of the most terrible yet fascinating periods in American history, filled with events that make truth seem stranger than fiction. In Geoffrey C. Ward's *The Civil War: An Illustrated History,* historians Ken and Ric Burns point out some incidents that make the study of the conflict so compelling.

As with any civil strife, the war was marked by excruciating ironies. Robert E. Lee became a legend in the Confederate army only after turning down an offer to command the entire Union force. Four of Lincoln's own brothers-in-law fought on the Confederate side, and one was killed. The little town of Winchester, Virginia, changed hands seventy-two times during the war, and the state of Missouri sent thirty-nine regiments to fight in the siege of Vicksburg; seventeen to the Confederacy and twenty-two to the Union.

Between 1861 and 1865, Americans made war on each other and killed each other in great numbers—if only to become the kind of country that could no longer conceive of how that was possible. What began as a bitter dispute over Union and States' Rights, ended as a struggle over the meaning of freedom in America. At Gettysburg in 1863, Abraham Lincoln said perhaps more than he knew. The war was about a "new birth of freedom."

But something else had come out of the upheaval as well. The nation had reshaped and revitalized itself, gained new insight into the meaning of sacrifice and suffering, and accomplished deeds mightier than anyone had dreamed possible. It had taken a step on the road to greatness, and life would never be the same again. One of the men who helped set it on that road, Abraham Lincoln, summed up the feeling. "Neither party expected for the war the magnitude or the duration which it has already attained. . . . Each looked for an easier triumph, and a result less fundamental and astounding. . . . [But] the Almighty has His own purposes."[5]

Chapter 1

The Statesmen

ike many Northerners, sixteenth president of the United States Abraham Lincoln had not believed that the country would ever go to war. To him, the United States was more than an ordinary nation, it was a proving ground for the notion that democratic government—a government of the people, by the people, and for the people—could work if given a chance. Thus, preservation of the Union was his paramount goal as he took on the task of leading his divided nation.

In contrast, leaders of the Confederacy supported the doctrine of states' rights, a policy that advocated limiting the rights and privileges of the federal government to powers expressly assigned to it in the Constitution. Believing that the United States was just a voluntary assemblage of states rather than an indissoluble Union, states' rights supporters felt that they could secede (withdraw) from the United States if they disagreed

with a federal law or felt that they were being unfairly treated in some way.

By the 1860s, many Southerners—including Jefferson Davis of Mississippi—felt that the federal government was overstepping its constitutional powers in trying to regulate the institution of slavery, specifically in passing the Missouri Compromise of 1820, the Compromise of 1850, and the Kansas-Nebraska Act of 1854. All three acts restricted slavery to a greater or lesser extent, and Southerners saw this as a serious threat to their rights, their freedoms, and their economy.

Jefferson Davis

Jefferson Davis, the tenth child of Samuel and Jane Cook Davis, was born on June 3, 1808, in Christian (now Todd) County, Kentucky. The family left the state and settled in Mississippi when Jefferson was still a baby, and there he attended a log-cabin school during his elementary years. He later went to Transylvania University in

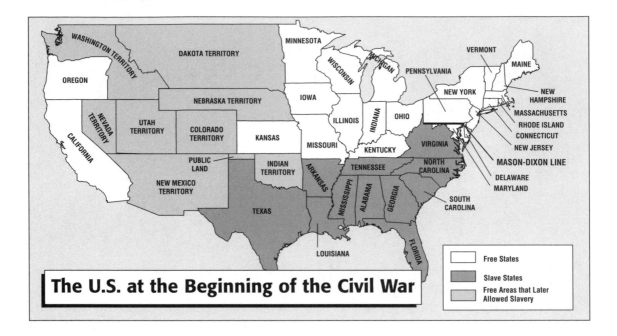

The U.S. at the Beginning of the Civil War

Legend:
- Free States
- Slave States
- Free Areas that Later Allowed Slavery

Lexington, Kentucky, and in 1824 entered the U.S. Military Academy at West Point. Some of his fellow students at the academy described him as serious, remote, arrogant, and self-satisfied, but Davis was not above having fun. In his second year, after flaunting the rules once too often, he was court-martialed and almost expelled. He managed to graduate in the bottom third of his class in June 1828.

After leaving West Point, Davis spent seven years on the frontier as a lieutenant in the U.S. Army, fighting Native Americans, building forts, and scouting. During this time he came to see himself as a military expert, and he began to develop a rigidity of character that would influence his leadership during the Civil War. Historian Burton J. Hendrick writes,

Davis loved routine, definite organization, obedience, deference to superiors, authority, gradation in position. . . . To give orders and have them obeyed; to look up to superiors and to keep those of lower rank in their appropriate place . . . such was his natural disposition, and army experience did much to intensify it.[6]

Davis's rigidity was reflected in his appearance. Tall, gaunt, tight-lipped, and impassive, with carefully combed brown hair and a well-starched collar, the Mississippian appeared cold and unapproachable, and he never earned the love of common people, as did Abraham Lincoln or Robert E. Lee. "[Davis is] the Sphinx of the Confederacy,"[7] one friend later commented.

Rising Politician

Davis left the military because of ill health in 1835 and became a planter in Mississippi. He married twice, to Sarah Knox Taylor in 1835, then, after her death, to

Tall, gaunt, and tight-lipped, Confederate president Jefferson Davis never earned the love of the people he governed.

Varina Howell in 1845. That same year he won a seat in Congress as a representative from Mississippi. Over the next fifteen years he also served in the Senate (taking time out to fight in the Mexican War in 1846) and as President Franklin Pierce's secretary of war, standing firm as a strong advocate of states' rights by opposing bills that limited slavery.

Like most Southerners of his time, Davis believed that slavery was justified since blacks had been "savages" in Africa, civilized only by Western society's influence. "We recognize the Negro as God's book tells us to recognize him—our inferior, fitted expressly for servitude,"[8] he stated. Davis's views were strengthened by economics. His growing wealth stemmed directly from slaves who worked the cotton fields on his sprawling plantation.

When Abraham Lincoln was elected president in 1860, and Mississippi joined other Southern states in seceding from the Union, Jefferson Davis resigned from the U.S. Senate. He hoped that his West Point experience qualified him to become head of the armies of the Confederacy, but instead he was named Confederate president in February 1861, with Alexander Stephens of Georgia chosen as vice president.

Disappointed, Davis conscientiously took on the enormous responsibility of leading an infant nation into war. "I had not believed myself as well suited to the office as some others. I thought myself better adapted to command in the field,"[9] he stated years later.

War President

Events would prove Davis right. He was not gifted as an administrative leader. Opinionated and, in the words of one observer, "as obstinate as a mule,"[10] he lacked people skills and regularly failed to consider points of view other than his own. Overly concerned with details, he allowed office seekers to constantly interrupt him, and he voluntarily dealt with mountains of daily paperwork—letters, reports, promotions, transfers, and complaints—that could have been taken care of by subordinates. "There is nothing too trivial for his attention," one visitor wrote, "and nothing escapes his notice."[11]

Although he wasted no time picking his cabinet, personality clashes and Davis's tendency to interfere too much with their decision making caused several members to resign. They were replaced with other men who were willing to give

Ships of the Desert

Prior to the Civil War, Secretary of War Jefferson Davis was a dynamic force, strengthening the army, introducing modern weapons, overseeing construction of military roads, and reinforcing coastal defenses. Having served on the frontier, he was interested in alternative means of transport in Southwestern deserts, and to that end he directed that camels be imported into the army in 1856. Author William C. Davis explains in *Jefferson Davis: The Man and His Hour.*

He never gave up on an idea once convinced of its usefulness. Even though some in the Senate had laughed in 1851 when he introduced his resolution to experiment with the "ship of the desert" in the American Southwest, he remained undeterred, and his position as secretary of war allowed him to put his idea to the test. In the fall of 1855 he sent a ship to Egypt, then to Turkey, charged with bringing back the odd beasts. Ten dromedaries came from the former and another forty-four from the latter. They all arrived in the spring of 1856, and Davis meanwhile devoted many of his evening hours to translating a French book on camels for the instruction of the animals' American handlers, who would be assisted by several Arabs hired to train them. . . . In the end the experiment withered and died from apathy after Davis left office. Soldiers disliked the ill-tempered beasts, preferring their horses and mules, and later the coming of the railroad preempted the need for them. Nevertheless the camels proved their effectiveness and adaptability; the timing of their introduction was simply unfortunate. Ironically, this one comparatively insignificant experiment, of much lesser importance than any of his efforts at modernizing weapons and instruction, would become the second-most-remembered episode in the life of Jefferson Davis.

in to the president's wishes rather than fight for their own convictions. Historian Shelby Foote writes, "He fell out [quarreled] with whoever did not yield to him in all things, and any difference was immediately made personal."[12]

Filling the War Treasury

Davis was a tireless worker, but he miscalculated and mismanaged when it came to weighty issues that affected the Confederacy. He counted on the fact that England would support the Confederacy in the war since England's textile industry relied heavily on Southern cotton. He expected English ships to break the sea blockade that Lincoln had imposed, thus allowing the South to receive vital war supplies from Europe. He also anticipated that European banks would provide loans that the Confederate government needed to keep running.

England, however, not only disapproved of slavery, but it had a surplus of raw cotton in its storehouses, had new sources of cotton in Egypt, and was hesitant to become involved in controversial American issues. Davis's hope for European support never materialized. Southern cotton rotted on docks and in storehouses, and Southerners had to make do with the few supplies that could be smuggled past the naval blockade by sleek, gray-painted blockade running ships that were fast enough to evade capture by Union vessels.

With little hope of European financial aid, Davis was left with few options for raising the necessary funds. States' rights supporters were categorically opposed to taxation by a centralized government, and there was no apparatus in place early in the war for assessing or collecting taxes. Davis thus resorted to borrowing, taking out loans from states and private citizens for the millions of dollars necessary to run the government and the war.

At first, the policy seemed to work well. "With plenty of money, we shall have no difficulty under your good management in whipping the Yankees,"[13] a Treasury agent reassured the president. But more was needed as the war proceeded, and soon the government was issuing promissory notes (IOUs) for everything it procured.

Davis also allowed his government to print paper money that was not backed by gold, silver, or anything of real value. Such a move helped lead to high inflation. In time, the government was bowed under by the weight of its debts, and Confederate money was so worthless that soldiers used it to line their shoes during the winter.

Attacked and Criticized

Davis's responsibilities were made more burdensome by attacks on his personal abilities and by obstruction to his policies that began almost immediately after he took office. He was accused of partiality in appointing government and military officials. (In fact, Davis did have a habit of appointing friends and cronies, then stubbornly refusing to remove them when they proved poorly qualified.) Governors such as Joseph Brown of Georgia and John Letcher of Virginia objected to any of Davis's decisions that seemed to appropriate state powers, such as his appointing officers over troops from their states. In his opposition, Brown went so far as to issue an executive order forbidding any firearms to be taken out of Georgia, so troops from that state were forced to leave for the war virtually unarmed.

Some of Davis's worst critics were men from his own cabinet. Secretary of State Robert Toombs complained before the First Battle of Bull Run, "Davis works slowly, too slowly for the crisis";[14] he resigned from his post before the end of July 1861 to enter the military. Secretary of War Leroy P. Walker resented Davis's interference in military decision making and resigned in the fall of that year. Vice President Stephens described Davis as a despot who disregarded the desires and aims of the Southern people. Early in the war, the vice president left the Confederate capital for his home in Georgia and spent the balance of the war criticizing the administration from a distance.

Davis met all such attacks stoically, showing the public a calm, impassive facade. Inside, however, he raged with hurt and anger, and the stress of such feelings affected his health, which had never been good. He was blind in his left eye (possibly from a chronic infection of a herpes

Confederate secretary of state Robert Toombs (pictured) did not respect Jefferson Davis, believing him to be too indecisive for the presidency.

simplex virus) and suffered from insomnia, recurrent fevers (possibly from malaria), and rheumatism. His wife described him as a "nervous dyspeptic by habit."[15] If he ate while upset or excited he was ill for days afterward. During the war, Davis's health broke repeatedly because of stress and hard work, but he carried on from his sickbed, pushing himself despite depression and severe "neuralgia" (pain) in his face and neck.

"A Blow at Constitutional Liberty"

Davis was overwhelmed by the numerous details involved in running the government, but he always took time for military affairs, because they were his true, overwhelming passion. Throughout the war, he appointed generals, removed others from command, and immersed himself in battle plans. (His most notable appointment was that of General Robert E. Lee as head of the Army of Northern Virginia.) Despite his responsibilities in the capital, he sometimes slept in the field with the army, and occasionally had to be removed from the battle zone by Lee's orders. "At the sound of guns, Mr. Davis was in the saddle and off, in a moment,"[16] recalled Davis's private secretary.

Introducing legislation to strengthen the army opened Davis to serious attack from his enemies, however. The army needed huge numbers of men, and to ensure that the burden of fighting did not fall "exclusively on the most ardent and patriotic," he pushed through the first draft law in American history in April 1862. Coming from the central government, it proved enormously unpopular. Governor Brown of Georgia declared that no "act of the Government of the United States prior to the secession of Georgia struck a blow at constitutional liberty so fell [deadly] as has been struck by the conscription [draft] act."[17]

Davis's decision to draft blacks into the Confederate army in the spring of 1865 also met with strong opposition.

Former secretary of state Toombs expressed the opinion of many when he wrote, "The worst calamity that could befall us would be to gain our independence by the valor of our slaves. . . . The day that the army of Virginia allows a Negro regiment to enter their lines as soldiers they will be degraded, ruined, and disgraced."[18]

Black Confederate soldiers drilled in the streets of Richmond in early 1865, but they never saw combat because the war ended shortly thereafter.

The Strain of Leadership

By the last year of the war, the problems Davis faced seemed continuous and overpowering. At home, he grieved over the death of his young son, Joseph, while facing calls for impeachment. On the war front, he watched helplessly while Union general William T. Sherman invaded Georgia, burned Atlanta, and then proceeded to lay waste the South. Union general Ulysses S. Grant and the Army of the Potomac was proving a match for Robert E. Lee, who was besieged at Petersburg, only twenty-five miles away from the Confederate capital of Richmond. In the North, Lincoln won reelection in November, ending Southern hopes that a new president would strike a bargain for peace with the Confederacy.

Davis would not admit it, but the Confederacy clearly could not hold out much longer. Farms and plantations were burned and plundered, cities were blackened ruins, transportation systems were disrupted. Even after the fall of Richmond on April 2, 1865, however, the Confederate president seemed to believe in the South's ability to win. "We have now entered a new phase of the struggle, the memory of which is to endure for all ages," he remarked. "Nothing is now needed to render our triumph certain but the exhibition of our own unquenchable resolve. . . . Let us but will it, and we are free."[19]

Despite his brave words, Davis fled Richmond and headed south with his family and a small group of cabinet members. On May 10, he was captured outside Irwinville, Georgia. The former president was transported to Fort Monroe, Virginia, where, manacled and humiliated, he awaited trial for treason against the United States.

Tragic Hero

Davis spent two years imprisoned at Fort Monroe. In May 1867, his wife succeeded in gaining his release after New York newspaper publisher Horace Greeley and a group of Northerners, hoping to speed reconciliation with the South, paid his $100,000 bail. Treason charges were dropped the next year.

Federal troops arrest Jefferson Davis after his escape from Richmond. Davis would spend two years in prison for treason against the United States.

Homeless, penniless, and physically broken, Davis and his wife returned to Mississippi and eventually accepted the offer of an admirer, Sarah Anne Dorsey, to take up residence in her home near Biloxi. There Davis worked for four years writing his memoirs, a two-volume work entitled *The Rise and Fall of the Confederate Government.* The book was not a financial success, being too expensive for impoverished Southerners to purchase and too dry, disorganized, and biased to attract many Northern readers.

Jefferson Davis died on December 6, 1889, of a bronchial infection and was buried in Richmond. Although he had been reviled for a time by Southerners because he failed to win the war, by the year of his death, many were acknowledging his contributions with gratitude and respect. In the end, Davis's patriotism and his willingness to sacrifice and suffer for the good of the Confederacy marked him as deserving of a level of recognition and remembrance that few Confederate statesmen merit.

Abraham Lincoln

Jefferson Davis's counterpart in government was Abraham Lincoln, born on February 12, 1809, near Hodgenville, Kentucky. Lincoln's parents, Thomas and Nancy, moved to Indiana in 1816, where Nancy died; Thomas then married Sarah Bush Johnston, a Kentucky widow. Lincoln later said of her, "All that I am I owe to my angel mother."[20] Lincoln received less than a year

of formal education in his youth, but he loved to learn and continued to study on his own throughout his lifetime. At first he read *Robinson Crusoe, Pilgrim's Progress,* and the Bible in front of the fireplace at night. In his twenties he studied law and debate. In his forties he tackled Euclidean mathematics and Shakespeare. When the war began he pored over books of strategy and talked to military experts until he was virtually an expert himself.

Congressman Lincoln

Lincoln became interested in politics and public affairs when he was a raw country boy of twenty-three living in Illinois. He made his first political speech wearing a straw hat, calico shirt, and pants held up by a single suspender. The impromptu address was short and to the point:

> Gentlemen and fellow citizens. I presume you all know who I am: I am humble Abraham Lincoln. I have been solicited by many friends to become a candidate for the legislature. My politics are short and sweet, like an old woman's dance. . . . If elected, I shall be thankful; if not, it will be all the same.[21]

Lincoln lost that election, but in 1834 he ran again and won. From then on, politics played a large part in his life, although he took time in 1842 to marry plump, temperamental Mary Todd. As a member of the Whig Party, he won a bid for Congress in 1846, but he lost popularity with party

Abraham Lincoln married plump, temperamental Mary Todd in 1842.

nois to serve only one term) and settled into law practice in Springfield, Illinois.

Lincoln became one of the most respected lawyers in Illinois, well known for his eloquence, honesty, and unassailable logic. He also gained increasing recognition for his powerful arguments against slavery. In October 1854, he spoke out against the Kansas-Nebraska Act, which created the territories of Kansas and Nebraska and allowed settlers of those new territories to decide for themselves whether or not they wanted pro-slavery governments. Lincoln challenged his listeners to consider whether slavery should be a part of any democratic government. "When a white man governs himself, that is self-government; but when he governs himself and also governs another man, that is more than self-government; that is despotism,"[22] he stated.

In 1858, Lincoln was nominated to run for the U.S. Senate and challenged his opponent, Stephen Douglas, to a series of debates. The debates fascinated Americans and brought out as many as fifteen thousand people at a time. Despite the impressiveness of Lincoln's arguments, he lost the election, and Douglas returned to the Senate for another term. Nevertheless, Lincoln had made a national reputation for

members after he outspokenly opposed the Mexican War. He left office in 1849 (it was the custom for Whig candidates from the Seventh Congressional District in Illi-

himself, and in 1860, the newly formed Republican Party nominated him to be its candidate for president.

Commander in Chief

Lincoln's views on slavery, his lack of enemies, and his humble background aroused great enthusiasm among Republican supporters. Since he faced divided opposition, he easily won the election with a majority of the electoral vote, although he did not win a majority of the popular vote and virtually no support from the South.

Lincoln assumed office on March 4, 1861, under some of the most terrific handicaps that ever hampered a president. Seven states had already seceded from the Union, and more were poised to go. The U.S. Army was daily losing Southern officers whose loyalty lay with their home states. War seemed imminent, and Congress endlessly debated the wisdom of compromising with the new Confederacy.

Lincoln refused to concede that a state had a legal right to secede. "It is safe to assert that no government proper ever had a provision in its organic law for its own termination. . . . No state upon its own mere motion can lawfully get out of the Union," he said, and issued a plea for unity to those who had broken away. "We are not enemies, but friends. We must not be enemies. Though passion may have strained, it must not break our bonds of affection."[23]

Despite Lincoln's pleas, war broke out on April 12, 1861, when Confederate forces fired on Fort Sumter in Charleston Harbor,

South Carolina. Congress was not in session in April when the fighting began, so Lincoln responded to the emergency by assuming powers not ordinarily granted to the executive. He directed that the writ of

A House Divided

Abraham Lincoln's "House Divided" speech, delivered on June 16, 1858, as he began his run for the Senate against Stephen Douglas, stands as a fine example of the simple, straightforward style that so appealed to ordinary Americans. A portion of that address is included in volume 1 of historian Shelby Foote's *The Civil War: A Narrative.*

If we could first know where we are, and whither we are tending, we could better judge what to do, and how to do it. We are now far into the fifth year since a policy was initiated with the avowed object and confident promise of putting an end to slavery agitation. Under the operation of that policy, that agitation has not only not ceased, but has constantly augmented. In my opinion it will not cease until a crisis shall have been reached and passed. "A house divided against itself cannot stand." I believe this government cannot endure permanently half slave and half free. I do not expect the Union to be dissolved—I do not expect the house to fall—but I do expect it will cease to be divided. It will become all one thing, or all the other. Either the opponents of slavery will arrest the further spread of it, and place it where the public mind shall be at rest in the belief that it is in the course of ultimate extinction, or its advocates will push it forward till it shall have become alike lawful in all the states, old as well as new, North as well as South.

habeas corpus be suspended so that known secessionists and disloyal persons could be held in prison without being charged with a specific crime. He distributed public funds to private agents to purchase arms and supplies. He ordered an increase in the size of the army and navy, requesting that seventy-five thousand men voluntarily enlist in the Union army immediately.

As commander in chief of the Union, Lincoln worked closely with his secretary of war to find the right man to lead the nation's armies into battle. This proved to be no easy task since many of the most promising generals were hesitant to lead or fight when given a position of authority. Until General Ulysses S. Grant was given supreme command in 1864, the president sometimes all but directed the war himself. He did not presume to manage the tactical moves of each battle, but he had a fine grasp of strategy and understood that winning the war involved breaking Southern morale rather than simply capturing Richmond, the Confederate capital.

"The Great Emancipator"

Lincoln entered the war with no intention of interfering with slavery in states where it already existed. He believed that slavery could be gradually eradicated without straining relations between slaveholders and nonslaveholders to the breaking point. He also hesitated to offend the governments of Missouri, Kentucky, and Maryland, border states that allowed slavery despite their loyalty to the Union.

As time passed, however, border-state loyalties became more certain, and Lincoln's determination to save the Union motivated him to reconsider his position on emancipation. Convinced that "a house divided against itself cannot stand,"[24] he decided that if the Union were to be preserved, it would have to embrace slavery or end it. Caution and compromise no longer seemed workable options. Lincoln prepared to issue a proclamation freeing the slaves as soon as the North won a decisive battle. He wanted the declaration to be seen as coming from a strong government, not a weak one.

The moment arrived in September 1862, after Union general George McClellan pushed Confederate general Robert E. Lee out of Maryland in the Battle of Antietam (Sharpsburg). The victory was limited, but Lincoln seized the opportunity to announce to the nation, and to the world, that on January 1, 1863, all persons held as slaves in states that had seceded from the Union would be granted their freedom. Slavery would continue to exist in those states that were loyal to the Union.

Lincoln's critics were quick to find fault with his Emancipation Proclamation, but most ordinary Americans, black and white, realized that an enormous first step toward ending a national injustice had been taken. "A poor *document*, but a mighty *act*," declared the governor of Massachusetts. Lincoln became known as "the Great Emancipator" and "the man who freed the slaves."[25]

Using the North's limited victory at the Battle of Antietam (pictured) as a sign of government strength, Lincoln issued a proclamation to free the slaves.

As a result of emancipation, almost 200,000 blacks fled the South, depriving the Confederacy of its labor. Many eventually served as soldiers in the Union army. The Emancipation Proclamation also ended the threat of European support for the Confederacy, since Europeans strongly opposed slavery and could not in good conscience fight against a nation that had taken a moral stand for human rights.

Eloquent Spokesman

Despite his awkward, unkempt appearance—he was 6'4", 180 pounds, with large hands and feet and a melancholy face—

Abraham Lincoln was a skilled and resourceful statesman and an eloquent spokesman. His decisions and directives—often expressed in witticisms, folksy anecdotes, and homespun stories—were straightforward, easily understood, and appreciated by ordinary people.

One of the most powerful examples of his eloquence was the Gettysburg Address, a speech delivered on November 19, 1863, at the dedication of the Gettysburg National

Cemetery, site of the most celebrated battle of the war. His remarks there became some of the most poignant and unforgettable words in history. Lincoln himself thought the address was a failure, but the principal speaker, orator and statesman Edward Everett, whose speech ran for hours, remarked, "I should be glad if I could flatter myself that I came as near the central idea of the occasion, in two hours, as you did in two minutes."[26]

Vote of Confidence

Throughout his administration, Lincoln was the subject of criticism and attacks from his own countrymen who believed he managed the war badly. Democrats felt that he was too extreme in his antislavery views and too rigid in his determination to reunite with the South. Radical Republicans saw him as too cautious, compromising, and ineffective.

Lincoln willingly tolerated partisan attacks, political maneuvering, even disrespect and humiliation if such tolerance helped lead to victory in the war. For instance, when General George McClellan, commander of the Army of the Potomac, pointedly insulted Lincoln and ignored his requests, the president told his secretary, "I

New Birth of Freedom

When Lincoln delivered his Gettysburg Address on November 19, 1863, he believed the speech to be a failure. Instead, his words have become some of the most famous in history. The address is taken from Geoffrey C. Ward's *The Civil War: An Illustrated History*.

Fourscore and seven years ago our fathers brought forth on this continent a new nation, conceived in liberty, and dedicated to the proposition that all men are created equal.

Now we are engaged in a great civil war, testing whether that nation, or any nation so conceived and so dedicated, can long endure. We are met on a great battlefield of that war. We have come to dedicate a portion of that field as a final resting place for those who here gave their lives that that nation might live. It is altogether fitting and proper that we should do this.

But, in a larger sense, we can not dedicate—we can not consecrate—we can not hallow—this ground. The brave men, living and dead, who struggled here, have consecrated it, far above our poor power to add or detract. The world will little note, nor long remember, what we say here, but it can never forget what they did here. It is for us the living, rather, to be dedicated here to the unfinished work which they who fought here have thus far so nobly advanced. It is rather for us to be here dedicated to the great task remaining before us—that from these honored dead we take increased devotion to that cause for which they gave the last full measure of devotion—that we here highly resolve that these dead shall not have died in vain—that this nation, under God, shall have a new birth of freedom—and that government of the people, by the people, for the people, shall not perish from the earth.

will hold McClellan's horse if he will only bring us success."[27]

McClellan criticized the president behind his back when Lincoln repeatedly urged him to fight the enemy in 1862. In 1864 the general ran against Lincoln in the presidential election, openly critiquing government policies and supporting a platform of compromise. Weary of war, the North seemed inclined to listen to McClellan and to blame the president for their problems. There had been no good military news for many months. The public appeared to favor a change of administration.

Despite everyone's expectations, however, when ballots were cast in November, Lincoln garnered 212 electoral votes to McClellan's 21. (Voters in Confederate states did not participate in the election.) The swing toward Lincoln was in part the result of news that Grant had finally forced Lee back to the defenses around Petersburg and Richmond and of General William T. Sherman's timely announcement that he had captured Atlanta in the heart of Georgia.

Still, the public had voiced their confidence in their commander in chief, and Lincoln was grateful. "I give thanks to the Almighty for this evidence of the people's resolution to stand by free government and the rights of humanity." He was also pleased that the nation had shown the world that "a people's government can sustain a national election in the midst of a great civil war."[28]

Planning for Peace

Not only did Lincoln concentrate on war matters during his presidency, but he planned for peace that he hoped would soon return to the troubled nation. From the beginning, the president was determined to be lenient in the terms under which rebellious Southern states would be restored to the Union. In his view, emancipation of the slaves and an oath of loyalty to the Union were the only prerequisites to reunion. When as little as 10 percent of the 1860 voting population had sworn loyalty to the Union, that state would then be readmitted to the Union.

Lincoln's proposal met instant objections from so-called radical Republicans in Congress who saw it as too tolerant. They wanted to punish their enemies by depriving them of their rights as well as their property. Thus, they drew up the Wade-Davis bill (sponsored by Senator Benjamin Wade and Congressman Henry Winter Davis), in which a majority of citizens in any state were required to swear loyalty to the United States before that state could be readmitted to the Union, and any man who had borne arms against the United States lost the right to vote. When presented with the bill to sign, Lincoln stuck it in his pocket and ignored it, thus ending discussion of the issue for the moment. The act, used by later presidents, became known as the "pocket veto."

Assassination

The war ended on April 9, 1865, when Confederate general Robert E. Lee surrendered his armies to Union general Ulysses S. Grant at Appomattox Court House in Virginia. Congress and the presidency were set for further conflict over reconstruction of the South when Lincoln was shot by actor John Wilkes Booth on the evening of April 14, 1865, while attending Ford's Theatre in Washington. Mortally wounded, Lincoln died the next day. "Now he belongs to the ages,"[29] said Edwin Stanton, who was at Lincoln's side when he drew his last breath.

Lincoln's body lay in the East Room of the White House until his funeral on April 19. His body was then transported by train to his hometown, Springfield, Illinois. Thousands lined the tracks, mourning the president's death as if they had lost a father or a dear friend. Lincoln was buried in what is now Lincoln's Tomb in the Oak Ridge Cemetery in Springfield. Orator and former slave Frederick Douglass expressed the nation's sentiments toward the great leader and spokesman for democracy when he said,

While attending a play at Ford's Theatre, Lincoln was shot by John Wilkes Booth. The president died on April 15, 1865.

His great mission was to accomplish two things: first, to save his country from dismemberment and ruin; and, second, to free his country from the great crime of slavery. . . . Dying as he did die, by the red hand of violence, killed, assassinated, taken off without warning . . . because of his fidelity to union and liberty, he is doubly dear to us, and his memory will be precious forever.[30]

Chapter 2

The Abolitionists

T he abolitionist movement gained national recognition in the United States in 1831, when William Lloyd Garrison began publishing his newspaper, *The Liberator*, in Boston, Massachusetts. The roots of the movement, however, could be traced to England in the 1780s, when statesman William Wilberforce and a group of wealthy evangelical Christians began speaking out against African slave traffic. Wilberforce's efforts were so successful that England outlawed the practice in 1807 and finally abolished slavery in the British West Indies in 1833.

Throughout U.S. history, American Quakers and some evangelical groups supported freeing slaves, and by 1804 Northern states such as Vermont, Massachusetts, and New York passed laws emancipating slaves within their borders. The abolition movement did not attract widespread attention, however, until western expansion began and pro-slavery pioneers demanded the right to carry their slaves with them into new territories. Appalled that such an evil would be perpetuated throughout the country, antislavery Northerners resisted, and the issue became hotly debated from private dinner tables all the way to the floor of the House and Senate.

Congress did its best to keep the conflict under control through a series of legislative compromises—the Missouri Compromise of 1820, the Compromise of 1850, and the Kansas-Nebraska Act of 1854. By the late 1850s, however, negotiation proved a failure, and the nation was deeply split over slavery. While some radicals like John Brown of Kansas went as far as taking justice into their own hands, more rational leaders, including William Lloyd Garrison and Frederick Douglass, used voices and pens to press for an end to the national evil.

William Lloyd Garrison

William Lloyd Garrison was born on December 10, 1805, in Newburyport, Massachusetts. His father was an alcoholic sailor

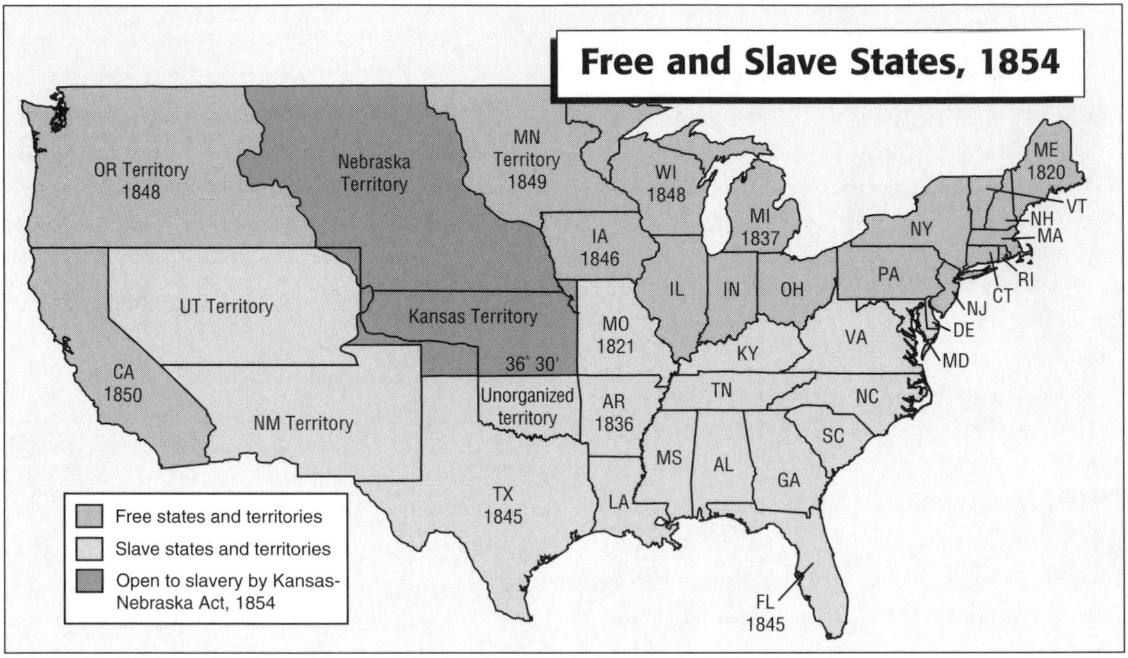
Free and Slave States, 1854
OR Territory 1848
Nebraska Territory
MN Territory 1849
WI 1848
MI 1837
ME 1820
VT
NH
MA
RI
CT
NJ
DE
MD
NY
PA
IA 1846
IL
IN
OH
UT Territory
Kansas Territory
MO 1821
KY
VA
CA 1850
36° 30'
Unorganized territory
AR 1836
TN
NC
NM Territory
SC
MS
AL
GA
LA
TX 1845
FL 1845
Free states and territories
Slave states and territories
Open to slavery by Kansas-Nebraska Act, 1854

who deserted his wife and children, and because the family needed money, William was apprenticed at the age of thirteen to the owner of the Newburyport *Herald* newspaper. He wrote of his first day of work:

> I never shall forget the surprise and amazement which I felt on first being led to the case to see the types set and distributed with such celerity [speed] by those who were familiar with the work, and my little heart sank like lead within me. It seemed to me that I never should be able to do anything of the kind.[31]

Garrison quickly learned the printing trade, however, and after completing his apprenticeship, he served as editor of several small newspapers in New England. Idealistic, determined, courageous, and deeply religious, he developed a passion for improving the world and wrote articles on the need for reforms of all kinds. He also condemned in print a variety of "evils," from theatergoing to war.

The Liberator

At age twenty-four, Garrison moved to Baltimore, Maryland—a center of slave trade in the United States—and began work with Benjamin Lundy, a Quaker and antislavery pioneer. The two men put out the weekly publication the *Genius of Universal Emancipation,* in which Garrison printed outspoken denunciations of slavery.

After one particularly scathing article that insulted a local slave trader, Garrison was sued for libel. He was tried, found guilty, and sentenced to a short term in prison, where he wrote numerous letters to friends, reassuring them of his willingness to suffer for a worthy cause. "How do I bear up under my adversities? I answer—like the oak—like the Alps—unshaken, storm-proof. . . . I will not hold my peace on the subject of African oppression. If need be, who would not die a martyr to such a cause?"[32]

Idealistic, determined, courageous, and deeply religious, William Lloyd Garrison founded the abolitionist journal The Liberator *in 1831.*

After his release from prison, Garrison moved to Boston, where he founded *The Liberator* in 1831. Although it was, in the words of biographer Walter M. Merrill, a "small, unimpressive-looking sheet, four pages, nine by fourteen and a quarter inches, with four columns to the page, . . . mild and colorless,"[33] it became one of the most influential journals in the United States at the time. Since Garrison hoped to attract a broad audience, the paper contained articles on a variety of topics such as smoking, drinking, the military, the clergy, the government, and cruelty to animals. His main thrust was the abolition of slavery, however, and his manifesto was plainly stated for all to read.

> I *will* be as harsh as truth, and as uncompromising as justice. On this subject I do not wish to think, or speak, or write, with moderation. . . . I am in earnest—I will not equivocate—I will not excuse—I will not retreat a single inch—AND I WILL BE HEARD.[34]

Garrison *was* heard, and he was soon hated by Southerners who believed his purpose was to incite rebellion and riot among the slaves. He received hundreds of abusive letters as well as threats on his life. Outraged city leaders denounced the paper and its editors. Southern vigilance societies offered rewards for the conviction of any person circulating copies of *The Liberator*. The Georgia House of Representatives did the same for anyone who arrested Garrison and brought him to trial.

Fearless Reformer

Even in the North, the radical publisher was an unpopular figure with some. In October 1835, an angry mob who disagreed with his antislavery stand dragged him through the streets of Boston until he was rescued and imprisoned for his own safety. On the wall of his jail cell, Garrison wrote, "Wm. Lloyd Garrison was put into this cell Wednesday afternoon, October 21, 1835, to save him from the violence of a 'respectable and influential' mob, who sought to destroy him

The front page of an issue of The Liberator. *The journal also included articles about smoking, drinking, the military, and the government.*

for preaching the abominable and dangerous doctrine that 'all men are created equal.'" [35]

Garrison's reaction to threats and violence was to fearlessly step up his efforts. He urged a boycott of slave-produced products in the North and advertised "free-produce" stores where cotton goods, tobacco, and sugar could be purchased. He urged the formation of antislavery societies and helped establish the first—the New England Anti-Slavery Society (later the Massachusetts Anti-Slavery Society)—in 1832.

The society had three aims: immediate emancipation; improvement of the lot of free blacks; and opposition to colonization, a scheme to transport free blacks out of the country and resettle them elsewhere. Despite its devotion to the cause of freedom, the society renounced the use of violence or revolt as a means of achieving freedom. At the close of the first meeting, Garrison remarked,

We have met to-night in this obscure school-house; our numbers are few and our influence limited; but, mark my prediction, Faneuil Hall [renowned town hall, meeting place of American patriots] shall ere long echo with the principles we have set forth. We shall shake the nation by their mighty power.[36]

The next year, Garrison helped establish the national American Anti-Slavery Society, made up of representatives from Massachusetts, Maine, Connecticut, and New York. He served as its president from 1843 until 1865. Of the two societies, the American Anti-Slavery Society was less radical; its members supported gradual emancipation, a process by which blacks would slowly achieve freedom and society

would be spared the economic and social upheaval resulting from immediate emancipation.

"Governed by Principles"

Garrison differed from many abolitionists in that, while they believed they could accomplish their ends through political means, he tried to remain apolitical, claiming, "I belong to no party in particular, but to all parties in general—in other words, I am not deceived or influenced by *names*, but governed by *principles*."[37]

The fiery publisher was not above taking a stand on political topics, however, and predictably, many of his stands were radical ones. He refused to vote, claiming that all political parties were tainted by pro-slavery elements. He refused to support the Constitution, claiming it was used to justify the continuation of slavery and was thus pro-slavery. Citing the motto "no union with slaveholders," Garrison called for the disunion of the nation, whereby the North would split from the South. "The Constitution . . . is an evil instrument," he asserted, "to be regarded with abhorrence by all good men. The Union, erected as it is on the prostrated bodies of three millions of the people, deserves to be held in eternal execration [hatred], and dashed to pieces like a potter's vessel."[38]

Garrison's opinions and demands were so radical and uncompromising that he was often involved in serious controversy even within the societies he supported. In 1840 he was part of a split in the

American Anti-Slavery Society, which resulted when some members wanted to support the newly formed Liberty Party and its presidential candidate, James G. Birney. That same year, he was outraged when the World Anti-Slavery Convention in London refused to seat women delegates. (Garrison was a strong supporter of equality of the sexes.) In the 1860s, strong personal differences between Garrison and another strong-minded leader, Wendell Phillips, again threatened to split the American abolitionist movement in two.

Garrison and War

Despite the controversy he stirred up wherever he went, Garrison was a pacifist, convinced that slavery should be abolished by moral, not physical, force. Even when attacked by an angry audience, he maintained a policy of nonviolence and was prepared to become a martyr for the cause if necessary.

As civil war neared, however, he had to reexamine those beliefs, particularly after John Brown's daring effort to free slaves at Harpers Ferry, Virginia, in 1859 resulted in the deaths of ten men. Garrison wrote,

> Was John Brown justified in his attempt? Yes, if [George] Washington was in his. . . . If men are justified in striking a blow for freedom, when the question is one of a three penny tax on tea, then, I say, they are a thousand times more justified, when it is to save fathers, mothers, wives and children

from the slave-coffle [chains] and the auction-block, and to restore to them their God-given rights.[39]

Garrison still believed that war could be avoided by disunion with the South, an act that would effectively eliminate slavery from the United States. Although disunion and secession were essentially the same—the end result would be two separate nations—he argued that disunion was morally justified because it was "based upon the eternal fitness of things and animated by a noble . . . and philanthropic spirit."[40] Secession was unjustified since it was motivated by the twin evils of slavery and states' rights.

Shortly after war broke out, Garrison modified his views on disunion and became an enthusiastic supporter of Northern efforts, perhaps seeing them as the most effective means of bringing an end to slavery. "Hail the approaching jubilee, ye millions who are wearing the galling chains of slavery; for, assuredly, the day of your redemption draws nigh, bringing liberty to you, and salvation to the whole land."[41] He cautioned friends and associates against criticizing the government since it was fighting the perpetrators of a depraved institution, and repeatedly reminded everyone that emancipation should not be overlooked in the fight to preserve the Union.

"A Great and Historical Event"

Never a moderate, Garrison was disappointed by the limited objectives of the

Emancipation Proclamation, issued by President Lincoln at the end of 1862, because it freed slaves only in Confederate states. Nevertheless, he soon recognized the decree as a significant step in the fight to end slavery and deemed it "a great and historical event, sublime in its magnitude, momentous and beneficent in its far-reaching consequences,

This Slavery-Cursed Union

In a speech delivered on the day of John Brown's execution, William Lloyd Garrison not only praised the radical abolitionist for the purity of his convictions, but he advocated that the North end slavery by disunion—secession—from the South. His speech can be found at *The History Place, Great Speeches* on the Internet.

We are living under an awful despotism—that of a brutal slave oligarchy [government by the few]. And they threaten to leave us if we do not continue to do their evil work, as we have hitherto done it, and go down in the dust before them!

Would to heaven they would go! It would only be the paupers clearing out from the town, would it not? But, no, they do not mean to go; they mean to cling to you, and they mean to subdue you. But will you be subdued?

I tell you our work is the dissolution of this slavery-cursed Union, if we would have a fragment of our liberties left to us! Surely between freemen, who believe in exact justice and impartial liberty, and slaveholders, who are for cleaning down all human rights at a blow, it is not possible there should be any Union whatever.

By the dissolution of the Union we shall give the finishing blow to the slave system; and then God will make it possible for us to form a true, vital, enduring, all-embracing Union, from the Atlantic to the Pacific—one God to be worshipped, one Saviour to be revered, one policy to be carried out—freedom everywhere to all the people, without regard to complexion or race—and the blessing of God resting upon us all! I want to see that glorious day!

William Lloyd Garrison praised John Brown (pictured) for the purity of his convictions and his efforts to end slavery.

and eminently just and right alike to the oppressor and the oppressed." When Congress voted to submit the Thirteenth Amendment to the states for ratification in February 1865, Garrison was exultant. "[This is an event] most important . . . in the history of congressional legislation, . . . better than all the military and naval victories of the war,"[42] he wrote in *The Liberator.*

As the war drew to a conclusion in 1865, Garrison believed that the work of abolitionists and antislavery societies was essentially finished. He called for their end, pointing out that great social changes were most successful when they had widespread popular support rather than only the championship of a small minority. "[Now] we have the million with us," he pointed out. "Let us mingle with the mass, then, and endeavor to work with the mass."[43]

Garrison did not have the power to end the movement unilaterally, but he did have control over *The Liberator*, and he shut down publication of the newspaper in December 1865. Now sixty years old, he continued to work for the New England Freedmen's Aid Society, which furnished teachers, books, and clothing to free blacks. He also continued to write articles and lecture on the freedman and his problems and became a supporter of free trade, justice for Native Americans, and women's rights.

Death of a Reformer

William Lloyd Garrison died of kidney failure at his home in New York on May 24, 1879. A rigid idealist who proved able to adapt to a tumultuous age, he is remembered as an outspoken advocate for reform and a passionate trailblazer who played an important role in the abolition of slavery. His colleague and old opponent Wendell Phillips said during his funeral address, "His was an earnestness that would take no denial, that consumed opposition in the intensity of its convictions, that knew nothing but right."[44] Civil rights leader Archibald Grimke took that acclaim one step further. "Garrison, more than any other man, embodied the moral forces of the conflict, the story of his life being essentially the history of the moral uprising against Slavery."[45]

Frederick Douglass

Frederick Douglass—renowned abolitionist, orator, and writer—supported the antislavery cause as passionately as William Lloyd Garrison, but for more personal reasons. Born Frederick Augustus Washington Bailey sometime in February 1817 on a plantation in Tolbert County, Maryland, Frederick was a slave, the son of Harriet Bailey and an unknown Caucasian father, possibly his master.

From his birth, Frederick experienced the harshness of the slavery system. Separated from his mother, he lived for a time with his grandmother, then joined other child slaves on the plantation, serving as errand boy and companion to the plantation owner's son. When he was seven or eight years old, Frederick went to live with a family in Balti-more, Maryland, and was lucky enough to be taught the funda-mentals of reading by his kindly new mistress. The lessons ab-ruptly ended, however, when his master learned of them and forbade further study.

This opposition, based on the notion that an educated slave was a worthless slave, only made learning more desirable to Fred-erick. "What he most dreaded, that I most desired. . . . In learn-ing to read, I owe almost as much to the bitter opposition of my master as to the kindly aid of my mistress,"[46] he later wrote. An ex-tremely bright and ambitious youth, Frederick secretly fur-thered his reading skills with the help of white children, and by studying newspapers, street signs, and the Bible.

Renowned orator and writer Frederick Douglass supported the abolitionist cause as passionately as William Lloyd Garrison.

Freedom!

By his midteens, Frederick had seen enough of the vast cruelties of slavery— separation of families, whipping, and even murder—to loathe the institution. Balti-more was one of the centers of slave trade in the United States, and he later wrote, "I've seen men and women chained and put on a ship to go to New Orleans and I still hear their cries."[47]

In 1836, when he was eighteen, Fred-erick was hired out to a shipbuilder in

Baltimore and became a caulker (one who makes a boat watertight by sealing the seams). A skilled and responsible workman, Frederick was gradually given a certain amount of freedom, and he used it to join the East Baltimore Mental Im-provement Society, where he furthered his education and developed debating skills. He also met and fell in love with a free black woman named Anna Murray, whom he married in 1838.

Creature comforts did not ease Frederick's discontent with his status, however, and in early September 1838 he slipped aboard a train heading north and escaped to freedom. "The chain was severed; God and right stood vindicated. I WAS A FREEMAN, and the voice of peace and joy thrilled my heart,"[48] he wrote. Frederick settled in New Bedford, Massachusetts, where Anna soon joined him. To celebrate his new life, he decided on a new name for himself, and was thereafter known as Frederick Douglass.

"A Thief and a Robber"

As a person who hated slavery, Douglass inevitably became involved in the abolitionist movement in New Bedford. Tall, broad shouldered, and handsome, with a thick mane of hair and piercing dark eyes, Douglass was asked to speak at an antislavery convention in 1841. His impromptu address revealed his rich baritone voice and his oratorical powers. "I stand before you this night as a thief and a robber. I stole this head, these limbs, this body from my master and ran off with them,"[49] he told his fascinated audience.

William Lloyd Garrison, one of the most prominent abolitionist leaders in the nation, heard Douglass speak that night and soon hired him as an agent of the Massachusetts Anti-Slavery Society. Although always in danger of being captured

and returned to slavery, Douglass became a traveling lecturer, speaking of his life as a slave and raising subscriptions to Garrison's abolitionist newspaper, *The Liberator.*

An overnight success as a speaker, in part because, as another society member noted, "The public had itching ears to hear a colored man speak and particularly a slave,"[50] Douglass took part in a six-month tour with Garrison in 1843. During his travels he was often treated roughly when he refused to sit in the "colored" section of trains, and he was sometimes attacked by pro-slavery supporters for his race and the message he carried. Nevertheless, he believed in his mission and continued to speak on the evils of slavery despite such opposition.

Author and Editor

During this period, Douglass continued his informal education until his polished manner and speaking skills were so impressive that listeners wondered if he was misrepresenting himself and his humble roots. Determined to vindicate himself, Douglass wrote and published the *Narrative of the Life of Frederick Douglass: An American Slave* in May 1845. It immediately became a best-seller, giving some of the details of his past and proclaiming to the world how slavery corrupts society and debases both slave and master.

Douglass's name soon became a symbol of liberty and achievement throughout the North, but his fame proved a threat to his freedom. Federal laws decreed that he

A Piece of Property

Frederick Douglass's first autobiography, *Narrative of the Life of Frederick Douglass: An American Slave*, contains a preface by editor William Lloyd Garrison. In the excerpt below, Garrison relates his feelings upon hearing Douglass speak for the first time, as well as his initial impression of the fugitive slave.

I shall never forget his first speech at the convention—the extraordinary emotion it excited in my own mind—the powerful impression it created upon a crowded auditory [auditorium], completely taken by surprise—the applause which followed from the beginning to the end of his felicitous remarks. I think I never hated slavery so intensely as at that moment; certainly, my perception of the enormous outrage which is inflicted by it . . . was rendered far more clear than ever. There stood one, in physical proportion and stature commanding and exact—in intellect richly endowed—in natural eloquence a prodigy—in soul manifestly "created but a little lower than the angels"—yet a slave, ay, a fugitive slave,—trembling for his safety, hardly daring to believe that on the American soil, a single white person could be found who would befriend him at all hazards, for the love of God and humanity! Capable of high attainments as an intellectual and moral being—needing nothing but a compara-

tively small amount of cultivation to make him an ornament to society and a blessing to his race—by the law of the land, by the voice of the people, by the terms of the slave code, he was only a piece of property, a beast of burden, a chattel personal, nevertheless!

Frederick Douglass's oratory skills impressed those who heard him, including William Lloyd Garrison.

could be returned to slavery if he were captured, so in the summer of 1845 he fled to England. For two years he remained in that country, speaking to enthusiastic crowds and enjoying the lack of racial prejudice among the British. With the help of friends, he raised the money needed to buy his freedom—$710.96—and was thus able

to end his constant fear of capture and reenslavement when he returned to America in early 1847.

Back in the United States, Douglass continued his speaking tours. Then in Rochester, New York, in the fall of 1847, he began publication of a weekly abolitionist newspaper, *North Star*, so called because escaping slaves often used the North Star as a point of reference when they fled northward to freedom. (The newspaper was called *Frederick Douglass' Paper* after 1851.) Douglass intended it to be a publication "under the complete control and direction of the immediate victims of slavery and oppression," since "he who has *endured the cruel pangs of Slavery* is the man to *advocate Liberty.*" [51]

After passage of the Fugitive Slave Act of 1850, Douglass also became involved in the Underground Railroad, a loose network of antislavery sympathizers who helped escaping slaves reach safety. He and Anna used their home in Rochester as an important station on the route. In 1855, he published

the second of his autobiographies, *My Bondage and My Freedom.*

"A War for and Against Slavery"

In 1859, as radical abolitionist John Brown put the finishing touches on his plans for a raid on the Federal armory at Harpers Ferry (now in West Virginia), he informed Douglass of his scheme, hoping to gain support for the projected slave uprising. Douglass was an acquaintance of Brown's and shared his abolitionist goals, but he refused

Federal troops capture John Brown at Harpers Ferry. Brown had asked Douglass for support of the raid, but Douglass refused.

to become involved, counseling the agitators against pursuing such a violent and disastrous course. After Brown's capture, Douglass feared reprisals and imprisonment and again fled to Europe for six months, returning to America in time to support Abraham Lincoln in the presidential election of 1860.

Lincoln was not an abolitionist, but he was morally opposed to slavery, and Douglass believed he stood a better chance of winning than other antislavery candidates did. When Lincoln's election led to war, Douglass was disappointed that the president's first priorities were to save the Union rather than to abolish slavery. "The American people and the Government at Washington may refuse to recognize it for a time, but the 'inexorable logic of events' will force it upon them in the end; that the war now being waged in this land is a war for and against slavery,"[52] he declared early in the conflict.

Douglass continued to push tirelessly for emancipation, and by the end of 1862, his labor was rewarded. Lincoln issued the Emancipation Proclamation in September, declaring that on the first day of the new year, all slaves held in rebellious states were to be free. Douglass described the effect of the president's announcement on thousands of blacks who gathered in Boston to celebrate.

The effect of this announcement was startling beyond description, and the scene was wild and grand. Joy and gladness exhausted all forms of expression, from shouts of praise to sobs and tears. . . . It was one of the most affecting and thrilling occasions I ever witnessed, and a worthy celebration of the first step on the part of the nation in its departure from the thralldom [bondage] of ages.[53]

Black Men in Uniform

Even before slaves were recognized as free human beings, Douglass encouraged the North to allow them to become soldiers in the national conflict. In an article published in 1861, he argued,

Is there the least reason to believe that a regiment of well-drilled Negroes would deport themselves less soldier-like on the battlefield than the raw troops gathered up generally from the towns and cities of the State of New York? We do believe that such soldiers, if allowed to take up arms in defense of the Government . . . would set the highest example of order and general good behavior to their fellow soldiers, and in every way add to the national power.[54]

To Douglass's satisfaction, Lincoln authorized black enlistment in the Union army early in 1863. The first regiment to form was the 54th Massachusetts, with Douglass himself assisting with recruitment. Two of the first men to enlist were his sons, Lewis and Charles.

Almost 180,000 black troops eventually fought for the Union, despite the fact

One of the almost 180,000 blacks who fought for the Union cause. Drummers such as this young soldier often preceded troops into battle.

that they received lower pay and faced discrimination and hostility from both sides. Nevertheless, most served faithfully and fought well throughout the war. As one trooper in the 5th Regiment Massachusetts Cavalry (Colored) testified, "The colored soldiers in this four years' struggle have proven themselves in every respect to be men."[55]

Conscience of the Nation

Because of book sales and speaking fees, Douglass was a well-to-do man by the end of the war, able to purchase for his family a gracious home overlooking Washington, D.C. Emancipation and the restoration of the Union did not bring an end to his work, however. He traveled and spoke on the need for equality for his people and for women's rights. He fought hard for passage of the Thirteenth, Fourteenth, and Fifteenth Amendments, which legally abolished slavery, granted full citizenship rights to blacks, and guaranteed blacks the right to vote, respectively. In a meeting of the Massachusetts Anti-Slavery So-

A New World

In all three of his autobiographies, Frederick Douglass described his feelings about gaining his freedom from slavery in 1838. In the third, the *Life and Times of Frederick Douglass*, published in 1881, he had had time to gain perspective and was able to relate in greater detail his tumultuous emotions when he began his life as a freedman.

> I have often been asked, how I felt when first I found myself on free soil. My readers may share the same curiosity. There is scarcely anything in my experience about which I could not give a more satisfactory answer. A new world had opened upon me. If life is more than breath, and the "quick round of blood," I lived more in one day than in a year of my slave life. It was a time of joyous excitement which words can but tamely describe. . . .
>
> Anguish and grief, like darkness and rain, may be depicted; but gladness and joy, like the rainbow, defy the skill of pen or pencil. During ten or fifteen years I had, as it were, been dragging a heavy chain which no strength of mine could break. I was not only a slave, but a slave for life. I might become a husband, a father, an aged man, but through all, from the cradle to the grave, I had felt myself doomed. . . . [Now] my chains were broken, and the victory brought me unspeakable joy.

ciety in 1865, he stated, "I am for the 'immediate, unconditional, and universal' enfranchisement of the black man, in every State of the Union. Without this, his liberty is a mockery; for in fact . . . if he is not the slave of the individual master, he is the slave of society."[56]

Douglass took time to write his third and most complete autobiography, *Life and Times of Frederick Douglass*, which was published in 1881. After Anna died in 1882, he fell in love with and married Helen Pitts, a white woman almost twenty years his junior. The marriage aroused a storm of criticism even among his children, who saw his marriage to a Caucasian as a repudiation of their worth as people of color. Douglass ignored the censure and contin-

ued to focus on issues he believed were more important to the nation.

Frederick Douglass died of a stroke in his home in Washington, D.C., on February 20, 1895, and was buried in that city. He is remembered as one of the most remarkable men in American history, as well as a great warrior in the battle for black equality. Professor of history John F. Marszalek says,

> It is fair to say that in many ways he was the conscience of the nation because he kept before the country the idea that this was a war, not just to bring the nation back together, but it was a war to end slavery, to bring equality to black people, and to make them part of American society.[57]

Chapter 3

Commanders of the Confederacy

Military commanders were some of the most notable leaders of the South during the Civil War, since the Confederacy lacked strong, charismatic statesmen whom the public could love and trust. Throughout the conflict, citizens directed their loyalty and devotion to generals such as Robert E. Lee and Thomas "Stonewall" Jackson, who became heroes, household names, and the authors of daring deeds that set the South cheering.

Robert E. Lee

Robert E. Lee, the most beloved Confederate leader of the Civil War, was born on January 19, 1807, in his ancestral home near Montross, Virginia. His family was an old and honored one. Diplomats and statesmen adorned the family tree. Robert's father, Henry "Light-Horse Harry" Lee, was a Revolutionary War hero, a friend of George Washington's, and a former governor of Virginia. Nevertheless, Harry

was a reckless man who wasted his fortune, and Robert felt the pinch of poverty as he grew up.

When he was seventeen, Robert Lee entered the U.S. Military Academy at West Point. Handsome, good-natured, and a hard worker, he was a popular cadet and a star pupil. He never earned a demerit (an achievement unmatched at the academy), was named adjutant to the corps of cadets in his senior year (West Point's highest honor), and in 1829 graduated second in his class as a member of the school's Army Corps of Engineers.

Virginia's Son

Lee married Mary Custis, great-granddaughter of Martha Washington, in 1831, and the couple eventually had seven children. He remained in the military, and when the Mexican War broke out in 1846, he took the opportunity to prove himself in battle. In 1859, he led the party of Marines that captured radical abolitionist

Robert E. Lee is cheered by his troops. Lee was the most beloved Confederate leader of the Civil War.

when Southern states began seceding from the Union in the winter of 1860–1861, he recommended that the Virginian head up the armies of the North. "Robert E. Lee is the greatest soldier now living, and if he ever gets the opportunity, he will prove himself the great captain of history,"[58] Scott said.

By the outset of the war on April 12, 1861, Lee had served in the U.S. military for thirty years, as an engineer, a soldier, and an administrator at West Point. Despite his long record of service, however, his love for and loyalty to his home state was stronger than his ties to the Union. Virginia seceded on April 19, and the next day, Lee resigned from the U.S. Army. "My husband has wept tears of blood . . . but as a man of honor and a Virginian, he must follow the destiny of his state,"[59] his wife explained.

Three days later, at the request of Virginia's governor, Lee accepted command of the state's armed forces and was promoted to the rank of major general. For a time he served as military adviser and troubleshooter for Confederate president Jefferson Davis, earning from his men the derogatory nicknames "Evacuating Lee" and "King of Spades," for his reliance on digging earthworks rather than assaulting

John Brown after his abortive raid at Harpers Ferry (now West Virginia). General Winfield Scott, general in chief of the U.S. Army, admired Lee so much that,

the enemy. In June 1862, he was placed in command of the Army of Northern Virginia after General Joseph E. Johnston was wounded in the Battle of Fair Oaks (Seven Pines). "The shot that struck me down was the best ever fired for the Confederacy,"[60] Johnston later wrote.

Audacity Personified

Lee's presence as head of the Army of Northern Virginia gave the South an enormous military advantage that it enjoyed throughout most of the war. Unexpectedly fierce, Lee pushed Union general George McClellan and his army back from Richmond in the Battles of the Seven Days in late June 1862 and sent them retreating down the Virginia Peninsula. In the Sec-

ond Battle of Bull Run (Manassas) on August 29, he swept General John Pope's forces from the field. At Fredericksburg, Virginia, on December 13, 1862, he repulsed General Ambrose Burnside, and on May 1, 1863, he unnerved General Joseph "Fighting Joe" Hooker and defeated him at the Battle of Chancellorsville.

Lee regularly went into battle with significantly fewer men than his opponents, but he was intelligent and insightful enough to pick the setting for his fights, to station his men so they could hit the

Federal troops are defeated by Lee's army at the Battle of Fredericksburg. Lee's inspired leadership gave the South a marked advantage over the North.

enemy at its weakest points, and to rely on the talents of his subordinates, many of whom were highly gifted fighters as well. Historian Robert K. Krick points out,

> Lee won because of his audacity and because he had skilled subordinates in James Longstreet and Stonewall Jackson. Lee did not interfere with them at the tactical level. Rather he placed Jackson in positions where he could launch a mighty attack and smash an army, and he placed Longstreet in situations where he could fight with unparalleled tenacity on the defensive. His strategies worked wonderfully well.[61]

Daring the Impossible

By the summer of 1863, Lee—now affectionately called "Marse Robert" (Master Robert) by his men—had won so many victories that he and his Army of Northern Virginia believed themselves to be almost invincible. Daring the impossible, the sixty-five-thousand-man force marched up the Shenandoah Valley into Pennsylvania in late June, hoping to intimidate the North and force it to sue for peace. The Army of the Potomac, now led by General George Meade, was in close pursuit, however, and Lee was caught unprepared at the little market town of Gettysburg, Pennsylvania, where the two armies faced off on July 1.

Not expecting to fight at Gettysburg, Lee did not go into battle with his usual advantages in place. The Federals (Union

Marse Robert

Despite his celebrity status during the war, Robert E. Lee remained an intensely private individual who shared his deepest feelings only with his family. As Geoffrey C. Ward points out in *The Civil War: An Illustrated History*, Lee's words and actions prove that his character conformed closely to his "perfect" public image.

"Can *anybody* say they know the General?" [Southern socialite and diarist] Mary Chesnut asked. "I doubt it, he looks so cold, so quiet, so grand." His natural dignity turned away too much familiarity. No one ever called him "Bobby Lee" to his face; his men favored "Uncle Robert" or "Marse Robert." Like his hero, Washington, he had a terrible temper, which he worked hard all his life to control. When he was angered, his cold stare was unforgettable. But he always referred to the Union army as "those people" rather than the enemy. "His house on the Pamunky River was burnt to the ground and the slaves carried away . . . " a friend noted, "while his residence on the Arlington Heights was not only gutted of its furniture, but even the very relics of George Washington were stolen from it. . . . Notwithstanding all these personal losses . . . when speaking of the Yankees, he . . . evinced (no) bitterness of feeling . . . but alluded to many of his former friends and companions amongst them in the kindest terms."

troops) had the better position, entrenched in the hills south of the town, and were able to fire down on Lee's men when the Confederates tried to attack. Confederate cavalry leader Jeb Stuart and his men, on whom Lee strongly relied to inform him of the strength and position of the enemy, had been detained on their way to link up with the main army in Pennsylvania. Without Stuart, Lee could not accurately move his troops to the best advantage to strike at the enemy's weak spots.

Finally, Thomas "Stonewall" Jackson, Lee's right-hand man whose skill and fearlessness had helped the Confederates achieve some of their greatest victories, had been killed in early May, and Lee was relying on subordinates who were not as incisive or as reliable. In fact, General James Longstreet repeatedly questioned Lee's strategy and tactics at Gettysburg and was slow in calling up his men during the battle. Lee failed to recognize how important Jackson had been to his success, and he came to grief when his other generals failed to measure up to standards Jackson had attained.

Disaster at Gettysburg

The Battle of Gettysburg lasted from July 1 through July 3, 1863. The first two days were bloody standoffs with both sides fighting valiantly but making little headway. The third, the climax of the engagement, ended in disaster for the Confederates. Lee struck at the center of the Federal line of defense, sending General George Pickett's thirteen thousand men on an ill-fated charge straight into the enemy guns. At the end of the assault, half of Pickett's men were dead or wounded, and surviving Confederates staggered back to their lines in disarray.

The attack demonstrated the hopelessness of a head-on assault over open ground against a strong enemy, and Lee never

Dead soldiers in the field at Gettysburg. Lee took full blame for the horrible loss of life at this Confederate defeat.

repeated the mistake. He did, however, assume full responsibility for the fiasco. "It is all my fault," he told his men, and later tendered his resignation to Jefferson Davis. "No blame can be attached to the army for its failure to accomplish what was projected by me. I am alone to blame."[62] Davis rejected the offer, and Lee retreated back into Virginia with his military might permanently weakened by his losses in the battle.

Grim and Bloody Warfare

By 1864, despite Lee's best efforts, Confederate military strength was deteriorating because of casualties, desertions, and a lack of reinforcements. Supplies were desperately short—men marched and fought barefoot, in tattered clothes, with empty bellies. In some cases, ammunition ran so short that they were forbidden to shoot except when it was absolutely necessary. Lee wrote to Richmond on April 7:

> I desire [General Robert F.] Hoke's & R. D. Johnston's brigades to be returned to me from North Carolina & Hanover Junction, & all the recruits that can be obtained. Supplies of all kind should be collected in Richmond or at points accessible to this army as rapidly as possible. With our present supplies on hand the interruption of the trains on the southern roads would cause the abandonment of Virginia.[63]

Resorting to such shifts, Lee was able to amass some sixty thousand troops, and he skillfully used them in a supreme effort to defeat Union general Ulysses Grant, the new commander of all Federal armies, beginning in May 1864. The two great generals pitted their skills against each other for the first time in the Wilderness, a desolate tangle of trees and undergrowth in northern Virginia. There, Grant commanded a force twice the size of Lee's, but was at a disadvantage since he was in unfamiliar territory and could not use his cavalry or artillery in the dense forest. Both sides fought fiercely, but neither could claim a victory. "Every advance on [the enemy's] part, thanks to a merciful God, has been repulsed. Our loss in killed is not large, but we have many wounded,"[64] Lee wrote to Secretary of War James A. Seddon on May 6, 1864.

The two armies were not finished with each other yet, however. Grant was tenacious, and Lee was willing to fight, since he believed that the Union general's enormous losses would eventually motivate the North to call an end to the war. Thus when Grant swung south toward the Confederate capital of Richmond, Lee quickly dropped back as well, and both sides raced for Spotsylvania Court House, a crossroads town north of the capital. Lee arrived first and was able to establish strong defenses from which his men fended off several heavy Federal attacks from May 8 through May 19.

Victory at Cold Harbor

With no definitive victory at Spotsylvania, Grant pushed southward again, forcing

Lee to take another stand even closer to Richmond. The armies met at Cold Harbor on June 3, and there Lee's long reliance on defense fortifications paid off, with disastrous results for the Federals. While Grant repositioned his forces in preparation for attack, the Confederates—skilled in digging trenches and building barricades—used the time to construct a seven-mile stretch of crisscross excavations in which they could be protected while they moved about and fired on the enemy from all directions. "Intricate, zig-zagged lines within lines, lines protecting flanks of lines, lines built to enfilade [fire upon] an opposing line, lines within which lies a battery, a maze and labyrinth of works within

works," [65] described one newspaper reporter who later visited the area.

From the Federals' perspective, the defenses appeared no different than others they had assaulted. When they charged the Confederate lines the next morning, however, they learned the difference. Over their strong defenses, the Confederates laid down a lethal barrage, killing and wounding five to seven thousand Federals in the first thirty minutes of the attack. "It was not war; it was murder," [66] one officer remem-

A burial detail at work after the Battle of Cold Harbor. Five to seven thousand Federals were killed or wounded in the first thirty minutes of fighting.

bered. The battle went down in the pages of history as one of the most destructive and profitless engagements of the Civil War, but it was one of Lee's easiest victories.

Dignified in Defeat

Lee had no opportunity to press his advantage after Cold Harbor. Undiscouraged by the defeat, Grant headed for the railroad center of Petersburg with the intention of seizing it and cutting supply lines to Richmond. Scrambling for position, Lee reached Petersburg first, only to be besieged by the Federals who forced the Virginian and his weary troops to defend the city for ten months. In September 1864 he wrote to Jefferson Davis, "Our ranks are constantly diminishing by battle and disease, and few recruits are received. The consequences are inevitable. . . . The time has come when no man capable of bearing arms should be excused."[67]

By now Lee understood that it was simply a matter of time before he and the Confederacy would be forced to admit defeat. In April 1865, he abandoned Petersburg to Grant and attempted a last desperate dash westward, hoping to eventually link up with the ragtag remains of Joseph Johnston's army in North Carolina. Grant's cavalry ruthlessly cut him off, however. "There is nothing left me to do but go and see General Grant," Lee told his staff, "and I would rather die a thousand deaths."[68]

Dignified in defeat, Lee surrendered his men to Grant at Appomattox Court House on April 9, 1865. After the meeting, the Confederate leader made a final ride down the lines on his famous horse Traveller, giving his men what comfort he could. "Men, we have fought the war together, and I have done the best I could for you. You will all be paroled and go to your homes."[69]

Private Citizen

After the war, Lee became a private citizen for the first time in almost forty years. He accepted the presidency of Washington College in Lexington, Virginia, where his dedication and expertise took the school to high levels of scholarship and prestige. Throughout his tenure, he urged both students and friends to relinquish feelings of bitterness and hatred they might cherish against the North. Looking back on the war, however, he said, "I did only what my duty demanded. I could have taken no other course without dishonor, and if it were to be done over again, I should act in precisely the same manner."[70]

Lee's achievements were unequaled in the war, and over time, his campaigns became models of strategy and tactics in military schools throughout the world. He gained fame for his ability to anticipate the actions of his opponents, for his skillful use of fortifications, and for his ability to command the field with a small body of entrenched troops.

Lee died peacefully after suffering a stroke on October 12, 1870, and was buried at Washington College in Lexington. A great and good man, who by his genius and devotion prolonged the war more than any other individual, Lee continues to be revered and respected to the present day. His daughter Mildred expressed the sentiments of the nation when she said after his death, "To me, he seems a Hero— & all other men small in comparison."[71]

Wise Adviser

Unlike many Southerners, Lee promptly applied for a pardon from the federal government after the war in order to regain his rights as an American citizen. His oath of allegiance was lost, however, and full citizenship was not restored during his lifetime. Despite this indignity, Lee retained a positive attitude that went far toward helping other Southerners overcome their bitterness, as historian Shelby Foote describes in *The Civil War: A Narrative*.

R. E. Lee encouraged all who sought his advice to take the loyalty oath required by the President's amnesty proclamation as a prerequisite to recovery of their rights as citizens, and even did so himself, barely two months after Appomattox, though nothing came of it then or later; he would go to his grave disfranchised. However, news that he had "asked for pardon" spread rapidly through the South, producing consternation, which was followed up for the most part, even among those who had been die-hards up till then, by prompt acceptance and emulation. "You have disgraced the family, sir!" ex-Governor Henry Wise sputtered when he learned that one of his sons had taken the oath. "But, Father," the former captain said, "General Lee advised me to do it." Taken aback, Wise paused only a moment before he replied: "That alters the case. Whatever General Lee advises is right."

Thomas "Stonewall" Jackson

A staunch supporter of Robert E. Lee, Thomas J. Jackson was born on January 21, 1824, in Clarksburg, Virginia (now West Virginia). Jackson's parents died when he was young, and the boy grew up in the country, living with a bachelor uncle who owned one of the largest farms in western Virginia.

Thomas had a relatively happy childhood. He attended school intermittently, hunted, fished, and made fiddles out of cornstalks, but he had a serious temperament and a hunger to improve himself. His father's shortcomings, particularly an addiction to alcohol, were a part of his family history, but Jackson was determined to make a mark for himself despite his flawed ancestry.

The Rigors of West Point

When he was eighteen, Jackson applied for entrance to the U.S. Military Academy at West Point, not because he dreamed of becoming a soldier but because he recognized that educated men were more successful than uneducated ones. Poorly qualified, Jackson was granted admission only after another applicant dropped out, and he set out for school, "a lean young man, standing about five feet ten with large hands and feet (said to be nearly a size fourteen), and ill-cut brown hair on a head that seemed a bit too large for his body."[72]

At West Point, more polished cadets made fun of the overly serious, gawky country boy, but Jackson ignored them and concentrated on his studies. They were

Poorly qualified for West Point, Stonewall Jackson nonetheless graduated in the top third of his class due to his dedication and hard work.

would work away at his lessons by the glare of the fire, which scorched his very brain, till a late hour of the night."[73]

During this time, Jackson began laying down personal rules that he believed would help make him a better, more successful man. "Endeavor to do well in everything you undertake"; "Sacrifice your life rather than your word"; and "You may be whatever you resolve to be,"[74] were just a few of them. Once Jackson settled on these "truths," he stuck to them sternly and rigidly, and the strict military discipline at West Point encouraged his inflexibility.

Jackson graduated from West Point in 1846 in the top third of his class, a tribute to his dedication and hard work. He remained in the military in the hope of making a name for himself, and he did so to some extent in the Mexican War, exhibiting the total indifference to danger that would earn him fame in the Civil War. At one point, when shot and shells were falling all around him and his men dropped their guns to seek shelter, he called, "See, there is no danger. I am not hit!"[75]

Jackson the Eccentric

A fearless warrior in battle, Jackson was at the same time keenly interested in religion and in his health. His obsessive, perfectionistic personality led him to go to

extremely difficult for him, and he put in long hours struggling to make passing grades. One student remembered, "He was always at his books." Another said, "[He would] pile up his grate with anthracite coal, and lying prone before it on the floor

extremes with both. A conscientious Bible student, he carefully monitored his every word, thought, and action to avoid accidental or intentional sin. He stopped reading or writing letters on Sunday and timed his mailings so that his letters would not travel on that holy day. He prayed without ceasing, explaining to an acquaintance, "I never raise a glass of water to my lips without lifting my heart to God in thanks and prayer."[76] In time, he joined the Presbyterian church, became a Sunday school teacher, and attended weekly prayer meetings without fail. Historian William C. Davis writes, "His was a religion of the Bible and the Bible taken literally."[77]

When he wasn't thinking about God, Jackson focused on his health. He suffered from a variety of physical infirmities—weak eyes, poor hearing, chronic indigestion—and also from some imaginary ones, such as a conviction that one arm was heavier than the other. To ease his real and fanciful pains, he followed many unusual practices that made him appear eccentric to those around him. For a time he restricted his diet to foods such as stale bread, plainly cooked meat, and water, even bringing them along when he was invited out to dinner. He stood tall or sat erect at all times to keep his digestive tract as straight as possible. He rode with one arm in the air to aid his circulation, and rumor had it that he sucked lemons, even in battle during the Civil War. Whenever possible, he followed a strict daily schedule that included a cold bath, strenuous exercise such as leaping or swinging his arms, and an early bedtime. He would abruptly leave a meeting or a friendly gathering in order to carry out the latter.

Despite his eccentricities, Jackson was courteous, well mannered, and comparatively handsome, and women found him attractive. He married twice—in 1853 and again, after his first wife's death, in 1857. From 1851 until 1861, he was a professor at the Virginia Military Institute in Lexington, where he proved to be a terrible instructor. His odd mannerisms caused the students to make fun of him. His clumsiness led to disaster during science experiments, and his lectures, which he memorized and recited by rote, were monotonous and unclear. If a student asked for an explanation, Jackson simply repeated what he had said before in exactly the same words. As one observer stated, he "never descended to the level of his pupils' understanding."[78]

A Legend Is Born

At the outbreak of the war, Jackson left teaching to join the army. He was commissioned a colonel (but would become a brigadier general in July 1861), assigned a brigade of Virginians, and sent to guard the Shenandoah Valley, a fertile stretch of land that lay due west of Washington.

Shortly after that, the qualities that would make him a legend began to surface. When Confederate general Pierre G. T. Beauregard called for reinforcements as he prepared to fight the First Battle of Bull Run (Manassas) in July 1861, Jackson responded instantly and unquestioningly. He eluded

Federal (Union) troops that blocked his path, rallied his men, and marched at top speed for two days, finally catching a train from Manassas Gap to the battlefield. Jackson's sweeping arrival, from some sixty miles away, in time for the battle was the first of many seemingly impossible maneuvers that the eccentric former professor would pull off during the course of the war.

On the battlefield at Bull Run, Jackson looked nothing like a professor. He stationed his men, now designated the

Old Blue Light

No man in the Civil War exceeded the eccentricity of Stonewall Jackson, a mighty warrior who trusted only God and Robert E. Lee. Jackson's uncanny dedication and single-mindedness is described by historian Shelby Foote in Geoffrey C. Ward's *The Civil War: An Illustrated History*.

[Jackson] had this strange combination of religious fanaticism and a glory in battle. He loved battle. His eyes would light up. They called him "Old Blue Light" because of the way his eyes would light up in battle. He was totally fearless, and had no thought whatsoever of danger at any time when the battle was on. And he could define what he wanted to do. He said, "Once you get them running, you stay right on top of them, and that way a small force can defeat a large one every time."...

He had a strange quality of overlooking suffering. He had a young courier, and during one of the battles Jackson looked around for him and he wasn't there. And he said, "Where is Lieutenant So-and-so?" And they said, "He was killed, General." Jackson said, "Very commendable, very commendable," and put him out of his mind. He would send men stumbling into battle where fury was and have no concern about casualties at the moment. He would march men until they were spitting cotton and white-faced and fell by the wayside. He wouldn't even stop to glance at one of them, but kept going.

Jackson would disregard the pain and suffering of his men during a battle.

First Virginia Brigade, in the best position for firing down on the enemy, then rode along the lines, his eyes blazing with excitement, ignoring bullets that fell all around him. When other Confederates started to panic, one commander managed to check their flight by pointing to Jackson and crying, "Look! There stands Jackson like a stone wall! Rally behind the Virginians."[79] Jackson and his men did indeed prove an unbreakable bulwark around which others rallied that day and from whom the Federals eventually broke and ran. The nickname "Stonewall" stuck, and it proved so apt and popular that it characterized Jackson for all time.

Most Valued General

Jackson excelled as a military man simply because he did not accept anything less than success from himself and his men. He believed that God was on the side of the Confederacy and that simple, unwavering belief obligated him and the men he commanded to do their best, whether that was marching, obeying orders, killing the enemy, or dying for the cause. He was stern, demanding, inflexible, and cold-blooded, but he was also awe-inspiring in battle because he was totally fearless and accomplished near-impossible feats that would have daunted other men.

In the spring of 1862, Jackson was again assigned to the Shenandoah Valley, and there he honed his fighting skills and made his reputation as a man who seemed to be in a hundred places at once. His main task was to keep forty thousand Federal troops occupied that would otherwise be sent to fight under Union general George McClellan in his Peninsula Campaign. Jackson fulfilled his assignment admirably. Ignoring meals and the need to rest, he marched his fifteen thousand men up to twenty-five miles a day, repeatedly striking at and then eluding his opponents. Historian Armstead L. Robinson writes:

> He would attack in the morning, attack in the evening, attack at night. The Union commanders complained that he had to have more soldiers than they had been told; the same group could not possibly be striking here, there, and over there. The result was that the Federals had to keep large numbers of troops in the valley in a vain effort to defend against an army that was actually much smaller than it appeared.[80]

In the course of one month, Jackson's men marched over four hundred miles, killed and wounded seven thousand Federals, seized large quantities of supplies, and threatened the safety of Washington itself.

Jackson did not pause after such heroic deeds in the Shenandoah Valley. In June 1862, he and his men were on hand to help Lee demoralize McClellan in the Battles of the Seven Days in Virginia. In August of that year, he helped bring about Union general John Pope's defeat at the Second Battle of Bull Run (Manassas).

Promoted to major general, Jackson became Lee's most valued general as the war progressed, playing a vital role in the Battle of Antietam (Sharpsburg) in September 1862, in the Battle of Fredericksburg in December 1862, and in the Battle of Chancellorsville in May 1863. His fierce resolution to carry out his assignments or die in the attempt helped the Army of Northern Virginia earn a reputation for invincibility. Although far from perfect—he had difficulty getting along with his fellow officers and subordinates, was poor at communication, and had no sympathy for his men's sufferings—he was highly popular because of his ability, audacity, and his triumphs. One man wrote,

> There is a magnetism in Jackson, but it is not personal. All admire his genius and great deeds; no one could love the man for himself. He seems to be cut off from fellow men and to commune with his own spirit only. . . . Yet the men are almost as enthusiastic about him as over Lee, and when he moves about . . . most men shout with enthusiasm.[81]

Triumph and Tragedy

Jackson's career came to an abrupt and tragic end midway through the war. On May 2, 1863, the Confederates wound up a day of hard fighting against Union general Joseph Hooker's army near Chancellorsville, in the wild region of Virginia known as the Wilderness. That day, Jackson had persuaded Lee to divide his army and allow Jackson to lead a sweep around the Federal right flank. It had been a desperate gamble, since Lee faced Hooker's seventy-three thousand men with only seventeen thousand of his own. Still, the plan had worked, and the Federals had been driven back in confusion.

As night fell, Jackson and several of his officers rode out between the two armies' front lines, reconnoitering for a possible night attack. Nervous about just such a possibility, sentries on both sides spied the shadowy figures moving through the darkness. Assuming the worst, they opened fire. The Confederate leaders reined their horses back to their own lines, but some of the bullets found their mark. Jackson was hit by his own men, who wounded him in the left arm. Two of his aides were killed outright.

Carried to a field hospital, Jackson's shattered limb was amputated the next morning. For a time, doctors were optimistic, but complications soon set in. The general developed pneumonia, and on Sunday, May 10, his doctor broke the news that he would not live out the day. "It is all right," Jackson replied. "It is the Lord's day; my wish is fulfilled. I have always desired to die on Sunday."[82]

"Terrible Loss"

On hearing the news of Jackson's death, Jefferson Davis declared a national day of mourning, and men and women across

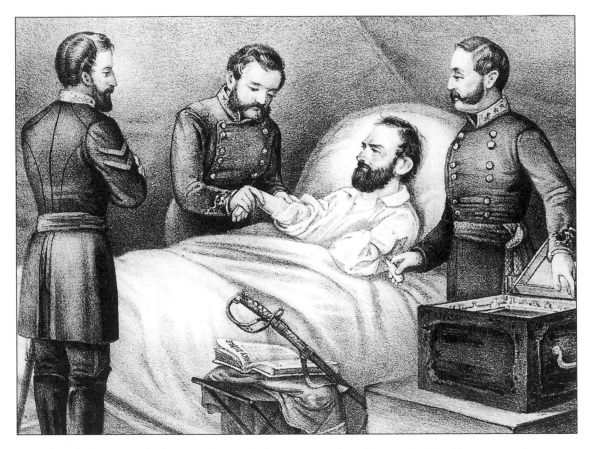

Accidentally wounded by his own sentries, Jackson lies in a field hospital after the amputation of his bullet-shattered arm.

the South lamented the passing of the great warrior on whom they had relied so strongly. Jackson was buried in Lexington, in what is today known as the Stonewall Jackson Memorial Cemetery.

Although his men petitioned to escort the body during the funeral, Lee refused, explaining that "those people over the river [the Union army] are again showing signs of movement,"[83] and reminding them that Jackson would never allow them to shirk their duty. On May 30, 1863, the First Virginia Brigade, Jackson's unit, was officially designated the Stonewall Brigade,

the only Confederate unit ever to have its nickname so recognized.

Some historians wonder whether, if Jackson had survived, he could have brought about Southern victories in later battles such as Gettysburg, and if his presence at Lee's side might have changed the outcome of the war. In all likelihood, one man could not have accomplished so much.

His death, however, proved to have serious long-term repercussions for the Confederacy. He was the single commander who had intuitively known what Lee wanted when going into battle. With Jackson as his "right arm," Lee had accomplished the impossible. After Jackson, there was no one so trustworthy, no one who challenged the enemy with the same ferocity of spirit. Lee spoke for the entire South when he said, "[His death] is a terrible loss. I do not know how to replace him."[84]

Chapter 4

Commanders of the Union

The North had the men and materials required to win the Civil War, but finding military leaders with the courage and determination to defeat the enemy proved difficult. Early commanders of the Union lacked the genius and daring of Confederate military men. Hesitant and shortsighted, they were inclined to spare their forces rather than push them on to ultimate victory.

After years of frustration, trial, and error, however, the North was finally able to find "fighting" generals, men who were willing to cope with the numbers of lives that had to be sacrificed in order to wear out the enemy and win the conflict. Two of the finest—Ulysses S. Grant and William Tecumseh Sherman—seemed among the least likely to achieve fame and glory when the war began in 1861.

Ulysses S. Grant

No one could have guessed that Ulysses Grant would become a hero in the Civil War. Named Hiram Ulysses at his birth on April 27, 1822, in Point Pleasant, Ohio, he grew up so quiet and reserved that he failed to correct registrars who listed him as "Ulysses Simpson" when he enrolled at the U.S. Military Academy at West Point in 1839. An indifferent student, he spent much of his time reading novels, and he graduated in 1843 with a commission in the infantry despite the fact that he loved horses and had a flair for working with them.

Uncertain Start

Grant remained in the military after graduation and served in the Mexican War in 1846. He later noted,

Besides the many practical lessons the Mexican War taught, it brought nearly all the officers of the regular army together. The acquaintance thus formed was of immense service to me in the war of the rebellion afterwards. For instance, I had known General [Robert

A failure at almost everything he tried in civilian life, General Ulysses S. Grant would become a hero during the Civil War.

After the Mexican War, Grant courted and married steady, reliable Julia Dent, then was sent to serve at an isolated army outpost in California. There, bored and lonely without his wife, he turned to alcohol, as he would do under similar circumstances during the Civil War. In 1854, he resigned from the army and settled in Missouri, where he set about trying to make a living as a civilian.

Supporting a wife and growing family proved difficult for a man who seemed to be a failure at everything he tried. He enjoyed farming, but he could not make a living at it and resorted to peddling firewood on the streets of St. Louis to make ends meet. He tried bill collecting, but was too unassertive to be successful. Finally, in the summer of 1860, he moved his family to Galena, Illinois, where he went to work in his father's harness shop.

Despite such setbacks, Grant never saw himself as a failure; in fact, he considered himself capable of greatness. His self-confidence, which few were astute enough to notice, and Julia's loyalty carried him through the hard times and the monotonous months in Galena. Then war was declared, and the government put out a call for troops. Unhesitantly, Grant offered his services to the army. "I

E.] Lee personally and knew that he was mortal, and it was just as well that I felt this.[85]

have but one sentiment now: that is we have a government and laws and a flag and they must be sustained. There are but two parties now: traitors and patriots. And I want hereafter to be ranked with the latter,"[86] he stated.

"Unconditional Surrender"

Although Grant was a West Point graduate, it was two months before he received a commission in the army; he was finally appointed colonel over a regiment of Missouri volunteers. Grant was proud of his men, however, and trained them until they were as proficient as veteran troops. On one of their first forays into Confederate territory, all learned a valuable lesson when they ran across an enemy encampment from which the men had fled at their approach. Grant wrote,

> It occurred to me at once that Harris [the Confederate leader] had been as much afraid of me as I had been of him. This was a view . . . I had never taken before; but it was one I never forgot afterwards. From that event to the close of the war, I never experienced trepidation upon confronting an enemy.[87]

Grant's confidence was also raised when he was promoted to brigadier general later that summer.

As the war continued, Grant began to prove his worth as a fighter and a leader of men. In September 1861, he captured Paducah, Kentucky, without firing a shot;

then in February of the next year he helped capture Fort Donelson in Tennessee, one of the first significant Union victories of the war. His refusal to compromise with the enemy and his insistence on unconditional surrender at Donelson earned him recognition as a hero. Delighted Northerners declared that his initials, U.S., stood for "Unconditional Surrender." Lincoln was pleased enough to promote him to major general.

Resolute Warrior

Though uninspiring as a civilian, Grant was direct, determined, and imperturbable when it came to military matters. Even when his army was badly beaten, he refused to admit defeat. Such was the case on April 6, 1862, when Grant and forty-five thousand men were caught off guard during a Confederate attack near Pittsburg Landing, Tennessee. The battle, which lasted for two days, centered around a small Methodist church called Shiloh Chapel and involved some of the fiercest fighting of the war.

At the end of the first day, the Confederates considered themselves victors and waited for the Federals (Union troops) to retreat. Grant, however, had other plans. When friend and subordinate William T. Sherman remarked, "Well, Grant, we've had the devil's own day, haven't we?" Grant answered laconically, "Yes. Lick 'em tomorrow."[88] He kept his word and forced the Confederates to withdraw by the end of the following day.

Grant was instrumental in the capture of Fort Donelson (pictured). Northerners said that his initials, U.S., stood for "Unconditional Surrender."

Casualties at Shiloh numbered more than thirteen thousand for the Union (ten thousand for the Confederates) and earned Grant a new nickname, "Butcher Grant." Many congressmen were critical of his fearful losses and demanded his recall after the battle, but Lincoln observed, "I can't spare this man. He *fights.*"[89] Not only did he fight, but he was quick to learn as well. After Shiloh, Grant was always on guard and never again assumed that the enemy would wait to attack.

For a time, Grant's effectiveness was hampered by political maneuvering among his superiors, but in October 1862, he was promoted to head the Army of the Ten-

nessee and began making plans to capture the heavily fortified city of Vicksburg, Mississippi, a Confederate stronghold on the Mississippi River. Grant worked for five months to take the town, while climate, terrain, and heavy artillery from the Confederates held him back. Finally, in an unconventional maneuver, he marched his men south, ferried them across the Mississippi, then advanced on Vicksburg from the southeast. Before reaching the town and besieging it, he fought five battles and managed to divide and weaken Confederate forces in Mississippi.

Once outside of Vicksburg, the Union navy shelled the town from the river for more than a month, while Grant's big guns hammered away on land. Finally, on July 4, 1863, the town's defenders declared defeat. "The long beleaguered, stoutly defended, and sadly punished city was ours at last, and it has ever since seemed to us, who shared in the glories of that day, that we had two Fourths to celebrate. One for our national birth, and one for Vicksburg,"[90] declared a Union chaplain.

Deceptive Demeanor

Despite his heroic accomplishments, Grant did not look or act like a hero. He was short, sturdy, and slightly stoop-shouldered with a square inexpressive face that made him look like "an earnest business man,"[91] as one visitor said. He smoked constantly and had a habit of whittling a stick into chips rather than letting his hands be idle. He dressed carelessly, disliked uniforms and marching bands, and claimed he could recognize only two songs: "One was Yankee Doodle, the other wasn't."[92]

Although considered a butcher on the battlefield, he always insisted that his meat be cooked well done, since even a hint of blood on his plate made him queasy. He was subject to migraine headaches and was sometimes moody and unsociable, explaining to his friend and chief of staff John Rawlins, "I don't

---

Hazardous Habit

After Ulysses S. Grant's victory at Fort Donelson, newsmen nicknamed him "Unconditional Surrender" Grant, and admirers sent him thousands of cigars to express their appreciation, as Bruce Catton describes in *Reflections on the Civil War*. Grant died of throat cancer in 1885.

Grant became a very famous and very popular man. Oddly enough, during the battle, the newspaper correspondents sent back to the Northern newspapers a dispatch telling how Grant rode along battle lines with a stub of a cigar clinched in his teeth. Grant had been a smoker, but he mostly smoked a pipe at that time. But something about that story—the image of a cigar in the teeth of the General on the firing line—struck the public fancy and the first thing Grant knew, he received from the North hundreds of boxes of cigars. He was a frugal man and hated to waste things, so he smoked them, and became a confirmed cigar smoker for the rest of his life.

Two years later, in the great Wilderness Battle, Grant was such a confirmed smoker that one of the officers on his staff told this story about him: At the start of the day's fighting, Grant in his tent reached into his possessions and stuffed all of his pockets full of cigars. The officer who watched him counted them, apparently, and said he had twenty-two cigars in the various coat pockets. That evening, just before dinner, Grant came back to his tent and a friend came up to him. Grant reached in his pocket to offer him a cigar and found that he had just one left. Twenty-one of them had been smoked during the day.

know whether I am like other men or not, but when I have nothing to do, I get blue and depressed."[93]

The Way Up

Because of his success at Vicksburg and his growing popularity with Lincoln and the War Department, Grant was assigned to head all the armies of the West in October 1863. Soon after, he headed for Chattanooga, Tennessee, where starving Union troops had been bottled up by Confederates since September. "When Grant arrived we began to see things move," one officer remembered. "We felt that everything came from a plan."[94]

Grant reestablished supply lines to the city, and in November, Federals and Confederates fought the Battle of Chattanooga. Grant's troops not only emerged victorious, but they were then well positioned to move into Georgia and split the eastern Confederacy in two.

In March 1864, Congress promoted Grant to lieutenant general, a rank previously held only by George Washington. It also gave him command of the entire Union army, which now numbered over 500,000, the largest in the world. Always practical, Grant chose to lead from the field, establishing mobile headquarters with the Army of the Potomac (led by General George Meade, who had commanded it since just prior to the Battle of Gettysburg in July 1863).

In May 1864, Grant began a coordinated offensive, in which all Union armies worked together to defeat the enemy. One of his key directives was to his most reliable general, William T. Sherman, who set out that summer to march through Georgia, seize Atlanta, and lay waste the heart of the South. Meade and Grant went after Confederate general Robert E. Lee's Army of Northern Virginia. "Wherever Lee goes, there you will go also,"[95] Grant told Meade.

No Turning Back

Grant first attacked Lee's forces in early May in the Wilderness of Virginia, where the Federals stumbled blindly through impenetrable forests, and the wounded burned to death in fires that swept through the undergrowth. Although his men were hard hit in that battle, Grant did not retreat but immediately moved south toward Richmond. His overall strategy was simple and based on a long-held premise. "One of my superstitions had always been when I started to go anywhere, to do anything, not to turn back or stop until the thing intended was accomplished."[96]

Lee fell back to protect the Confederate capital, and the two armies clashed again near Spotsylvania Court House, then farther south at the dusty crossroads of Cold Harbor, where, on June 3, Grant misjudged Lee's defensive capabilities and lost seven thousand men in the first thirty minutes of battle.

Cold Harbor was a debacle that Grant would always regret, but he nevertheless forged ahead with his plan to defeat Lee, besieging him and his army for ten months at Petersburg, Virginia, a railroad and supply link between Richmond and the rest of the South. It was a long, dis-couraging standoff, with soldiers living in trenches, plagued by flies, sun and rain, shelling and mortar fire. "Our matters here are at a deadlock; unless the Rebs

Hastening the End

The concept of total warfare—war waged against civilians as well as soldiers—was unpopular with many generals in the Civil War, but it proved effective in un-dermining the Southern economy and Southern morale. In volume 1 of Robert Underwood Johnson's *Battles and Leaders of the Civil War*, Union general Ulysses S. Grant explains the circumstances that motivated him to use such ruthless tactics against the enemy.

Up to the battle of Shiloh, I, as well as thousands of other cit-izens, believed that the rebel-lion against the Government would collapse suddenly and soon if a decisive victory could be gained over any of its armies. . . . But when Confed-erate armies were collected which not only attempted to hold a line far-ther south . . . but assumed the offensive, and made such a gallant effort to regain which had been lost, then, indeed, I gave up all idea of saving the Union except by complete con-quest. Up to that time it had been the policy of our army, certainly of that portion com-manded by me, to protect the property of the citizens whose territory was invaded, without regard to their sentiments, whether Union or Secession. After this, however, I regarded it as humane to both sides to protect the persons of those found at their homes but to con-sume everything that could be used to sup-

Grant succeeded because he was willing to cripple the South to win the war. Here, his troops destroy Confederate supplies and railroad tracks.

port or supply armies. . . . Supplies within the reach of Confederate armies I regarded as contraband as much as arms or ordnance stores. Their destruction was accomplished without bloodshed, and tended to the same result as the destruction of armies. I contin-ued this policy to the close of the war. . . . This policy, I believe, exercised a material influence in hastening the end.

commit some great error they will hold us in check until kingdom come,"[97] declared one Federal soldier.

Generous in Victory

Lee inevitably had to give up his defense of Petersburg, however. The Confederate army was badly weakened by disease, losses on the battlefield, and a lack of food and supplies. On April 2, 1865, outnumbered almost five to one, it began its retreat with Grant's Federals in pursuit. Richmond also fell on April 2, and finally, on April 9 near the little crossroads town of Appomattox Court House, the conflict drew to a close. Lee sent a message to Grant, asking to meet and discuss terms of surrender. Grant, who had been suffering from a terrible migraine all day, felt relief from pain "the instant I saw the contents of that note."[98]

The two men met in the parlor of Wilmer McLean; some of the first shots of the war had crashed through McLean's home near Manassas four years before. Lee arrived in his best uniform and well-polished boots. Grant, whose baggage had gotten lost several days before, wore a rumpled, muddy uniform and looked, according to one of his men, "rather dusty and a little soiled."[99]

Grant greeted Lee graciously, tried his best to put him at ease, and composed the terms of surrender clearly and rapidly. "When I put my pen to the paper, I did not know the first word I should make use of in writing the terms. I only knew what was in my mind, and I wished to express it clearly so that there could be no mistaking it."[100]

Grant exhibited his greatness in the generous terms he offered—demanding essentially that officers and men surrender their guns and return to their homes. He allowed them to keep their sidearms and horses, which would be invaluable for spring planting, and distributed food rations, since most were starving. "I felt like anything rather than rejoicing at the downfall of a foe who had fought for so long and valiantly and had suffered so much for a cause,"[101] he stated.

Lee surrenders to Grant at Appomattox Court House.

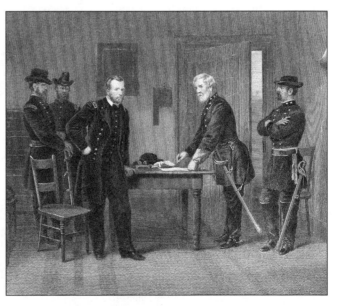

President Grant

Except for the formalities, the war was over. Grant sent a message to Washington announcing the victory. He was hailed by the nation as a hero, and four years later he was nominated for president of the United States. Winning easily, he promised to support peace, honesty, and civil rights. Instead, his administration was racked by scandal, and he lived with the knowledge that the war had freed the slaves but had not won equal rights for them.

In later years, unfortunate investments left Grant virtually penniless, and the general turned to writing his memoirs to renew his family's resources. In his account of the war, he stated, "I feel that we are on the eve of a new era, when there is to be a great harmony between the Federal and Confederate. I cannot stay to be a living witness to this prophecy, but I feel it within me that it is so."[102]

The general was not speaking in the abstract when he referred to his passing. He finished his work just days before dying of throat cancer on July 23, 1885. He was buried in Central Park, then in 1897 his remains were moved to a newly built mausoleum, Grant's Tomb, in Manhattan.

General Philip Sheridan, one of Grant's subordinates, later wrote of Grant, "There was no other soldier in the world who demonstrated the ability to wield such a huge machine as the Union army and to bend it to the mighty purpose of winning the war. That was Grant's great achievement."[103] Remembered as a simple, earnest, "ordinary" man, Grant's extraordinary talent for war indeed earned him an everlasting place in the annals of military history.

Dying of throat cancer, Grant works on his memoirs to restore his family's finances.

A good student at West Point, William Tecumseh Sherman was prone to carelessness.

William Tecumseh Sherman

One of the most astute military men of the Union, William Tecumseh Sherman was born on February 8, 1820, in Lancaster, Ohio, the sixth of ten children of a state supreme court justice who died when his son was nine years old. Shortly thereafter, the family split up, and William was taken

to live with Ohio senator Thomas Ewing, who treated the boy as an adopted son, sent him to some of the best schools in the state, and enrolled him in the U.S. Military Academy at West Point in the spring of 1836.

Early Career

Sherman proved a good student at West Point, proficient at chemistry, mathematics, and drawing. The lanky, redheaded cadet accumulated demerits for carelessness, however, and remained a private throughout his entire four-year career. He graduated sixth in his class in 1840 and served in the military for another ten years, despite the fact that he did not particularly enjoy army life.

In 1853, Sherman and his wife, Ellen Ewing, daughter of his foster father, moved to San Francisco to begin a banking career. That enterprise soon failed, and they relocated to Kansas, where Sherman joined his brothers-in-law in a new law practice. Unsuited for law, Sherman moved on, and his next endeavor was more to his liking. He became the first superintendent of the newly established Louisiana Seminary of Learning, a military academy that would later become Louisiana State University. The work there, which ranged from administration to carpentry, exactly suited his energy, creativity, and intelligence, and his interest in his students made him a beloved leader. "The magnetism of the man riveted us all to him very closely,"[104] observed one of the professors.

"Crazy" Sherman

By early 1861, war and secession were popular topics in the South. When Southerners talked of the war as if it would be a short skirmish with a decided end, Sherman warned them,

> This country will be drenched in blood. God knows how it will end. . . . You people speak so lightly of war. You don't know what you are talking about. . . . You mistake, too, the people of the North. They are peaceable but earnest and will fight.[105]

As Louisiana left the Union, Sherman resigned from his job and returned to his family in St. Louis, Missouri. Although he vowed that he would have nothing to do with the war when it broke out on April 12, 1861, he enlisted in May, accepting an assignment to hold the border state of Kentucky for the Union.

There, as he dwelled on the size and might of the enemy, he grew anxious and depressed, worried aloud to anyone who would listen, and demanded 60,000 men for support, 200,000 if he were asked to invade Tennessee. The figures sounded astronomical, and some observers reported that he was irrational, insane, and unfit for

duty. "Sherman is gone in the head,"[106] George McClellan declared. Close to a nervous breakdown, the Ohioan was sent east for a time to rest and recover.

By the end of 1861, Sherman had improved enough to return to active duty. He was assigned to serve under Union general Ulysses S. Grant in Kentucky, and the two men became close friends. Sherman would later say, "[Grant] stood by me when I was crazy, and I stood by him when he was drunk; and now, sir, we stand by each other always."[107]

Southern Assignment

In April 1862, Sherman played an important role with Grant in holding back the Confederate push in the Battle of Shiloh (Pittsburg Landing). "He dashed along the line, encouraging his troops everywhere by his presence, and exposing his own life with the same freedom with which he demanded they offer theirs,"[108] said one observer. He was also part of Grant's victorious force at Vicksburg and Chattanooga in 1863.

After Grant was promoted to lieutenant general and given command of all Union armies in March 1864, Sherman became head of all the armies of the West and was assigned the task of invading the South. Grant directed him "to move against [Confederate general Joseph E.] Johnston's army, break it up, and get into the interior of the enemy's country as far as you can, inflicting all the damage you can against their war resources."[109]

No longer anxious or depressed,

Sherman and his 100,000-man force set out from Chattanooga, Tennessee, on May 5, 1864, with Atlanta, Georgia, as their first objective. The Union commander had little time to spare on formalities such as clean uniforms and correct manners. His troops—unrefined Midwesterners and rough mountain men—would have scorned such affectations anyway. Instead, they and their leader focused on practicalities.

Every man carried five days' rations and plenty of ammunition. Sherman included in his supply train "dark wagons" in which engineers could make copies of maps they drew of the region, canvas pontoons for temporary bridges, and crews to repair telegraph and railroad lines that had been previously destroyed. After their use, his men again disabled the lines and pried up tracks, ensuring their permanent destruction by heating and twisting the iron into mangled shapes dubbed "Sherman's neckties."[110]

On the Offensive

As he moved through Georgia, Sherman practiced a flanking type of warfare—moving around the enemy force and hitting it from the side—rather than going head-to-head with Joseph Johnston's army, which continually tried to block his path. Repeatedly he forced the Confederates to fall back, and his army made steady progress, although it did not move fast enough for the restless, sharp-spoken commander. "A fresh furrow in a plowed field will stop the whole column," he cried. "We are [supposed to be] on the offensive and . . . must assail."[111]

Although always peevish and even eccentric, Sherman was at his best when under pressure. Such was the case in mid-June, when he and his army were on the outskirts of Atlanta. Panicky Confederate president Jefferson Davis replaced Johnston with General John Bell Hood, an intrepid warrior whom Davis believed would prevent the city's capture. The two armies engaged in a series of battles that ended with Hood's taking refuge inside the city. Sherman promptly sealed it off and for five weeks held it under siege, bombarding it continually. "[I] will push forward daily by parallels, and make the inside of Atlanta too hot to be endured,"[112] he wired Washington.

On September 1, Hood and his troops fled Atlanta, and Sherman's men marched in. "Atlanta is ours and fairly won,"[113] he triumphantly announced. The city, shelled for weeks on end, was a shambles, and Hood's retreating Confederates added to the destruction by blowing up several factories and trains to prevent their capture.

Sherman completed the ruin two months later. Rather than leaving men behind to hold the city, he set about destroying its manufacturing and military capabilities. Rails were torn up, telegraph wires were cut, and fires were set, which soon devoured the city's foundry, oil refinery, freight warehouses, theaters, stores,

A house damaged during the five-week bombardment of Atlanta. Sherman wanted to make the inside of the city "too hot to be endured."

and slave markets. "We have utterly destroyed Atlanta," wrote one Indiana soldier. "It's pretty hard . . . but it is war."[114]

Sherman did not take time to watch the burning. On November 16, while the city still smoldered, he and his men set out again on the second leg of their journey, heading deep into the interior of Georgia. Their mission was to cut a sixty-mile swath of destruction from Atlanta to the Atlantic Ocean. "If the North can march an army right through the South, it is proof positive that the North can prevail," he told Grant before he left. "I can make this march and make Georgia howl."[115]

Total War

The trek, which one of his men described as "a vast holiday frolic,"[116] had been carefully planned by Sherman. Studying census records and area maps, he marched his men through the richest farmland and past military targets that needed destroying. To be unhindered by demands from his superiors, he deliberately broke all communication with Grant and Washington. He also cut his supply lines, pointing out that if Georgians could live off the land, his men could too.

Parties of foragers, nicknamed "bummers," were put in charge of finding food and supplies for the army as it traveled. With few restraints, they pillaged, plundered, ransacked, and burned everything in their path, stealing silver and money, breaking dishes, destroying oil paintings, smashing pianos, and performing other random acts of violence. Sherman did what he could to

Angel of the Lord

Sherman shared many Americans' racial prejudices, and he discouraged the attendance of thousands of blacks who proclaimed him savior and followed his army on its march through Georgia and the Carolinas. Sherman worried that the presence of such civilians would undermine his success, as he recounts in his book, *The Memoirs of General W. T. Sherman.*

> I walked up to a plantation-house close by, where were assembled many negroes, among them an old, gray-haired man, of as fine a head as I ever saw. I asked him if he understood about the war and its progress. He said he did; that he had been looking for the "angel of the Lord" ever since he was knee-high, and, though we professed to be fighting for the Union, he supposed that slavery was the cause, and that our success was to be his freedom. I asked him if all the negro slaves comprehended this fact, and he said they surely did. I then explained to him that we wanted the slaves to remain where they were, and not to load us down with useless mouths, which would eat up the food needed for our fighting-men; that our success was their assured freedom; that we could receive a few of their young, hearty men as pioneers; but that, if they followed us in swarms of old and young, feeble and helpless it would simply load us down and cripple us in our great task. . . . I believe that the old man spread this message to the slaves, which was carried from mouth to mouth, to the very end of our journey, and that it in part saved us from the great danger we incurred of swelling our numbers so that famine would have attended our progress.

Blacks followed Sherman's army to seek protection. Sherman worried that they would impair his progress.

stem the violence, but he was inclined to overlook much of it, saying, "This may seem a hard species of warfare, but it brings the sad realities of war home to those who have been directly or indirectly instrumental in involving us in its attendant calamities."[117]

Sherman's strategy was known as "total war." Its onslaught not only broke the morale of Southern civilians but also weakened the Confederate army as thousands of soldiers deserted and returned to their homes in the hopes of protecting their families from Sherman's raiders.

In late December, Sherman's sixty-thousand-man army (he had sent a portion of his troops back to Tennessee to guard that state against Confederate attack) arrived on the Atlantic coast and captured Savannah. Sherman presented the city to Lincoln as a Christmas present, and the announcement delighted war-weary Northerners, who claimed the Ohioan as their newest hero.

On the third leg of his march, Sherman pushed northward into South Carolina, braving mud and winter weather to wage war against the state that many Northerners saw as the initiator of the Civil War. His men marched ten miles a day, cutting down trees to make roads, burning fences and barns, leaving nothing but rows of chimneys as witnesses of their passing. In Columbia, the state capital, on February 17, 1865, buildings and bales of cotton were set ablaze, and the city itself went up in smoke. One woman wrote, "On every side [was] the crackling and devouring fire, while every instant came

the crashing of timbers and the thunder of falling buildings. A quivering molten ocean seemed to fill the air and sky."[118]

The War Is Over

Three days later, on February 20, the Federals moved out of Columbia and continued their relentless march into North Carolina, where the destruction continued. Thirty-five miles out of Raleigh, the state capital, Sherman was met by Joseph Johnston, who had again been placed in command of Confederate forces. The two armies clashed, but Johnston, with just twenty thousand men left in his ragged army, was forced to retreat. "Sherman's course cannot be hindered by the small force I have," Johnston wired to Lee. "I can do no more than annoy him."[119]

Sherman's army set out again around the tenth of April, always moving northward, but their progress was broken almost immediately when a courier arrived with the news that Lee had surrendered to Grant at Appomattox Court House, Virginia, on April 9. Raleigh, the capital of North Carolina, capitulated to the Federals on April 12, and on April 17, Sherman and Johnston met near Durham to arrange Johnston's own terms of surrender.

The war was over, and Sherman was, in the words of the *New York World*, "the idol of the day."[120] The campaign had solidified the Ohioan's reputation as a brilliant strategist who attained his military objectives quickly and efficiently. With surprisingly few casualties, he had destroyed millions of dollars worth of property and goods, hastened the end of the war, and helped bring the South to its knees.

Sherman generously gave full credit for victory to his men as he bade them farewell in Washington in May 1865.

You have been good soldiers, so in peace you will make good citizens; and if, unfortunately, new war should arise in our country, "Sherman's army" will be the first to buckle on its old armor, and come forth to defend and maintain the government of our inheritance.[121]

More Perfect Peace

Sherman remained a hated figure to many Southerners long after the war, but he was respected and admired in the North, and he served as commanding general of the army from 1869 until 1883. Despite many calls to enter politics, he repeatedly rejected the notion, stating categorically that "I will not accept if nominated and will not serve if elected."[122]

Sherman died of complications from asthma, a lifelong ailment, on February 14, 1891, and was mourned nationwide. He was held in such regard that even his old opponent Joseph E. Johnston served as a pallbearer at his funeral. A sentence ascribed to Sherman on a statue in Washington reads, "The legitimate object of war is a more perfect peace."[123] That phrase sums up the philosophy of a unique man whose determination was surpassed only by his love for his country.

Chapter 5

The Cavalrymen

The Confederate cavalry played a visible and crucial role throughout the entire Civil War. Its members possessed fine horses, were experienced riders, and were fortunate to be led by skillful, dynamic, and inspiring men such as J. E. B. Stuart and Nathan Bedford Forrest.

In contrast, the Union cavalry was a relatively ineffective force for the first two years of the conflict. Older, high-ranking army officers failed to understand the importance of a mounted force and hesitated to spend money strengthening existing regiments. Government contractors hired to procure horses were incompetent or unscrupulous, so cheap mounts rather than healthy ones were the rule. Cavalry recruits were often "city boys" who were more afraid of their horses than they were of the enemy. Only with hard work, reorganization, and bold, innovative leadership were such shortcomings corrected and failures turned into ultimate success.

J. E. B. Stuart

Legend in the South and menace to the North, James Ewell Brown Stuart was the ideal to which hundreds of Confederate cavalrymen aspired during the Civil War. Born in Patrick County, Virginia, on February 6, 1833, he studied languages, history, and mathematics as a youth, then entered the U.S. Military Academy at West Point in July 1850. There he met and developed a friendship with its new superintendent, future leader of the Confederacy Robert E. Lee.

Stuart graduated from West Point in 1854 and became a cavalry officer in the West, where he patrolled for Native Americans, tried to keep peace between pro- and antislavery forces in Kansas Territory, and met and married Flora Cooke in 1855. In 1859, under the command of Robert E. Lee, he helped capture radical abolitionist John Brown at Harpers Ferry, Virginia (now West Virginia). Stuart remained in the U.S. Army until the outbreak

A legend in the South and a menace to the North, J. E. B. Stuart was considered to be the ideal cavalryman.

felt loyalty to his state. His oft-repeated statement was, "I go with Virginia."[124]

"Beauty"

Stuart began his war service commanding a regiment of cavalry near Harpers Ferry in May 1861. A great horseman and a talented leader, he set about instructing his men in proper cavalry procedures and in practical wisdom he had picked up in earlier days. Because Stuart always prepared carefully before setting out on an assignment, never asked anyone to do what he would not do himself, and treated his men as his equals, they admired and trusted him. "We learned to hold in high regard our colonel's masterly skill in getting into and out of perilous positions," one of his men wrote. "Before we reached Manassas, we had learned, among other things, to entertain a feeling closely akin to worship for our brilliant and daring leader."[125]

Part of Stuart's attractiveness was due to his charm, high spirits, and energy. He was a man who was inclined to laugh and sing even when going into battle. Not considered handsome—his classmates at West Point jokingly called him "Beauty"—his bright blue eyes and soldierly bearing nevertheless gave him distinction. He was

of the war in April 1861, when he resigned to join Virginia's forces as a colonel. He did so not out of strong political convictions but simply because he

easily recognizable by the gold braid and buttons that decorated his jacket, by the scarlet-lined cloak and yellow sash that billowed behind him, and by the gold spurs that twinkled on his boots. One ob-

The Grand Romantic

Although Jeb Stuart is often remembered as a happy-go-lucky romantic who overlooked the grim realities of war, the dashing cavalryman had a very practical side. Author Emory M. Thomas focuses on Stuart's depth and pragmatism in *Bold Dragoon*.

If Stuart dreamed and fantasized about the future . . . he also tried to prepare [his wife] and himself for the possibility that he might not have a future. "Bear in mind that if I fall I leave in the sacrifice thus made a legacy more to be prized by my children & you Dearest than 10 years of longer life.". . . In November he made his will and the following spring he purchased a $10,000 life insurance policy.

Stuart, the grand romantic, seemed to have few illusions about his life and the outcome of the war. He told [fellow cavalryman] George Cary Eggleston, "I regard it as a foregone conclusion . . . that we shall ultimately whip the Yankees. We are bound to believe that, anyhow; but the war is going to be a long and terrible one, first. We've only just begun it, and very few of us will see the end." Significant in this statement was Stuart's clear-eyed realism about his likely death and most revealing was his comment, "We are bound to believe that, anyhow." Stuart was aware that victory might be a matter of believing in victory and even if his cause were doomed, he knew that he had to believe otherwise in order to function.

server admiringly described "the brown hat with its black plume floating above the bearded features, the brilliant eyes, and the huge moustache, which curled with laughter at the slightest provocation."[126]

Women loved him, and he enjoyed flirting with them, but always discreetly, since he was devoted to his wife. His dashing facade masked the fact that Stuart was an experienced, professional soldier who understood what his cavalry should do and who could perform as well as or better than any of his men.

Harassing the Enemy

After helping lead the rout of the Union army in the First Battle of Bull Run (Manassas) in July 1861, Stuart was promoted to brigadier general. He and his men earned national recognition for their three-day, one-hundred-mile ride around Union general George McClellan's enormous Army of the Potomac as it lay encamped north of Richmond in June 1862.

Knowing that the Federal (Union) cavalry was a fragmented force that the Confederates could outfight or outrun, Stuart dared to plunge deep into enemy territory to get firsthand information on McClellan's troop dispositions (arrangements) for Robert E. Lee. After disrupting Federal supply and communication lines, Stuart returned unscathed with a fresh supply of horses and mules and information that helped Lee defeat the Federals during the Battles of the Seven

Days later that month. The North was humiliated, and Stuart became a hero to adoring Southerners who now began calling him "Jeb."

A month later, Stuart and fifteen hundred men raided Union general John Pope's headquarters about ten miles south of Manassas, Virginia, and managed to wreak havoc while getting away with a list of Pope's troop strength and dispositions. Historian Emory M. Thomas writes,

> The Southerners were everywhere. They cut telegraph wires. They fell among the Union troops and took ample advantage of the element of surprise. . . . [They captured] Pope's uniform and personal baggage, along with his dispatch book and money chests containing $500,000 in greenbacks and $20,000 in gold. . . . In addition to booty, the Confederates carried off more than 300 prisoners.[127]

With information about Pope's troops, Lee knew when and where to strike the Federals, and the Confederates were able to achieve victory at the Second Battle of Bull Run (Manassas) in late August. By then, Stuart had been promoted to major general and was given command of all the cavalry of the Army of Northern Virginia.

Mounted Force

Stuart made two more circuits around the Union army, first in October 1862 and again in December of the same year, capturing horses and mules and destroying enemy property. During the third raid, from behind enemy lines, he telegraphed the following message to the Union quartermaster general in Washington. "Next time I capture some of your mules, supply better mules. These are kind of worn out."[128] The incident delighted the South and provided further humiliation to Federal forces.

Stuart was not only a raider and reconnaissance man for Lee, however. He understood the importance of cooperating with the infantry, and he skillfully used his horsemen to carry out traditional operations usually assigned to a mounted force. He and his men served as scouts when Lee's army was on the march, feinting and skirmishing with the enemy to distract them and keep them from discovering Lee's movements. In battle—and Stuart participated in most major battles in the Eastern theater—his men protected the army's flanks. During a retreat, they guarded its rear from assault by Federal forces.

Brandy Station

By 1863, the Federal cavalry had improved its leadership, training, and performance, and Stuart faced stronger opponents than he had earlier in the war. Northern strength was demonstrated at Brandy Station, Virginia, in June 1863, when Stuart was surprised by eleven thousand Federal cavalrymen led by General Alfred Pleasonton, commander of General Joseph Hooker's cavalry corps.

The Federal attack at Brandy Station, Virginia, caught Stuart by surprise. Stuart claimed victory because Federal losses were greater than his.

Involved in putting on a "grand review" of his cavalry on June 8, Stuart's attention had been momentarily diverted from the war. Thus he was slow to respond when the Federals attacked early on the morning of June 9. Once aware of the grave danger, he responded with all his forces, and the cavalry battle that ensued was the largest ever fought in North America. One Confederate veteran wrote, "It was what we read of in the days of chivalry. Acres and acres of horsemen sparkling with sabers, dotted with brilliant bits of color when their flags danced above them. Hurled against each other full speed and meeting with a shock that made the earth tremble." [129]

In the end, hundreds of men and horses lay dead in the field. The Confederates lost five hundred men, but Stuart claimed victory because Federal losses were even greater and Pleasonton had been forced to withdraw. Some Southerners blamed Stuart for needless slaughter of his men, however, and even saw the battle as a Northern victory of sorts since it boosted the Federal cavalry's confidence in itself and allowed it to participate more actively later in the war.

Tardy at Gettysburg

Despite his embarrassment at Brandy Station, Stuart effectively screened the movements of Lee's army as it moved north on its invasion of Pennsylvania in late June 1863. On July 1 through 3, 1863, Lee would come head-to-head with Union general George Meade at Gettysburg, Pennsylvania, in the most monumental battle of the Civil War.

Unaware of what lay ahead, Lee gave Stuart permission to break away with his cavalry once they entered Maryland. The cavalryman had orders to collect supplies as well as information that could be vital to the success of Lee's invasion. Stuart began his move north in good order, but he soon encountered obstacles that prevented him from reuniting with Lee for over a week.

He had difficulties getting his men and artillery across the rain-swollen Potomac River, and he captured 120 wagons full of Federal supplies, which slowed his progress. Several times he encountered and fought with Federal cavalry.

When Stuart finally rejoined his commander, Lee was in Gettysburg and had been fighting for two days, hampered by the fact that Stuart was not there to give him vital intelligence regarding the enemy's position and strength. Pardonably angry at his subordinate's tardiness, Lee

The absence of Stuart's cavalry hurt the Confederate army at Gettysburg. Lee had no means of determining the enemy's position and strength.

reportedly said brusquely, "Well, General Stuart, you are here at last."[130]

Mortified, Stuart did his best to make up for lost opportunities. On July 3, he commanded a division of men who took part in fighting on the extreme left of the Confederate line. Although the day itself ended in defeat for the Confederates, Stuart reestablished his fighting reputation as he helped Lee and his army retreat to safety after the battle. During ten days of nonstop riding and skirmishing, he and his men protected supply wagons and ambulances while harassing Federal cavalry that tried to further destroy the infantry as it wearily marched south.

Stuart received much criticism and bad press for his late arrival at Gettysburg. One of Lee's staff suggested a court-martial, and the general himself, always loath to criticize, stated, "The movements of the army preceding the battle of Gettysburg had been much embarrassed by the absence of cavalry."[131]

Disaster at Yellow Tavern

Despite his failures at Brandy Station and Gettysburg, Stuart remained a powerful and highly respected force in Lee's army, someone against whom the feisty new leader of the Union cavalry, Philip Sheridan, was eager to prove himself. After getting permission from Union general Ulysses S. Grant, whose forces were assailing Lee's from the Wilderness to Cold Harbor in May and June 1864, Sheridan and more than ten thousand men set out toward Richmond, hoping

to draw Stuart away from Lee and out into the open where he could be attacked.

The plan worked. Stuart and forty-five hundred troopers took off after Sheridan. Riding hard, the Confederates reached an abandoned inn called Yellow Tavern on May 11, just hours ahead of Sheridan's Federals. Around noon, Sheridan arrived, and furious fighting ensued. In late afternoon, as the Federals made a mounted charge, Stuart rallied his troops for a countercharge, yelling "Give it to them, boys!"[132] A moment later he was shot.

His men helped him to an ambulance, and Stuart was transported away from the battle. Although wounded and weak, when he saw some Southern soldiers leaving the field, he called to them, "Go back! go back! and do your duty, as I have done mine. . . . Go back! . . . I had rather die than be whipped."[133]

Death of a Cavalier

Stuart was taken to Richmond, where doctors found that the bullet had pierced his lower abdomen and lodged there. Suffering but calm, he said, "Well, I don't know how this will turn out; but if it is God's will that I shall die, I am ready."[134] He succumbed to his wound the next evening and was buried in Richmond on May 13. No military display was possible, since all available troops were in the field, but cannon booming on the none-too-distant battlefield served as a salute to his passing. The loss of Stuart, the gifted professional, proved a terrible setback for

Lee and a stunning blow to Southern morale. His death removed one more prop from under the already shaky Confederacy, which collapsed less than one year later, on April 9, 1865.

Stuart's name has long conjured up visions of the romantic cavalier of yesterday, but he has earned a position in the annals of the Civil War as someone of greater significance as well. Historian William C. Davis explains:

> Stuart was . . . an innovator. He combined the gathering of intelligence and the masking of his army's movements with destruction and sabotage behind enemy lines. . . . [He] did far more than cavalry had ever done before, and . . . deserves to be remembered as an effective, imaginative soldier and not just as the man with a feather in his hat. [135]

Nathan Bedford Forrest

One of the best but most controversial cavalrymen on both sides of the war was Nathan Bedford Forrest, born near Chapel Hill in Bedford County, Tennessee, on July 13, 1821. Raised in poverty, Forrest worked hard to support his family—his father died when he was sixteen—and he spent what little spare time he had at such typical Southern pastimes as hunting, fighting, horse racing, and gambling. There was little time or thought spared for education. A former teacher wrote, "Bedford had plenty of

Nathan Bedford Forrest was one of the best but most controversial cavalrymen on both sides of the war.

sense, but would not apply himself. He thought more of wrestling than his books; he was an athlete." [136]

Bedford's uncle gave him his first opportunity in life when he invited his nephew to join him in his horse-trading business. By 1846, Forrest had married and was making money selling cattle, horses, and slaves. With the proceeds, he purchased property in Tennessee, Mississippi, and Arkansas. By the war's beginning in 1861, he was a wealthy planter who owned three thousand acres of land and forty-two slaves, and was a leader of his community. Most wealthy slave owners believed that the slave trade was an unworthy occupation for a gentleman, but Forrest was unapologetic, since he treated his "property" decently and viewed the business as an opportunity to make money to support his family comfortably.

Let's "Kill Some Yankees"

Forrest felt a degree of loyalty to the Union, but at heart he was a pro-slavery man. When Civil War broke out and Tennessee seceded on June 8, 1861, Forrest joined Captain Josiah White's cavalry unit, the Tennessee Mounted Rifles, as a private. Recognizing his potential as a leader, the governor of Tennessee soon authorized him to raise a regiment of cavalry (which Forrest did at his own expense) and promoted him to the rank of lieutenant colonel. Forrest went about the recruiting process enthusiastically. "Come on boys, if you want a heap of fun and to kill some Yankees,"[137] he promised in an appeal to one batch of recruits.

To Forrest, war was exciting. He was a man of action, and violence had been a fact of life since his youth. By the time he was twenty-four, he had killed a man to avenge his uncle's murder, and he thought nothing of killing the enemy in a legitimate war. Unlike some commanders, he fought on a personal level—preferring pistols, shotguns, and sabers over

artillery attacks—and always made sure he was in the front lines so that he knew what was going on. His call to battle was, "Forward, men, and mix with 'em."[138]

During the war, Forrest was wounded four times in battle, had twenty-nine horses shot out from under him, and killed at least thirty men in hand-to-hand combat. "I was a horse ahead at the end,"[139] he reputedly said.

Forrest did his fighting in the Western theater of the war between the Mississippi River and the Appalachian Mountains, engaging Federal (Union) troops in Tennessee, Alabama, Kentucky, and Mississippi. He took part in the Battle of Shiloh (Pittsburg Landing) in April 1862 and in numerous lesser-known battles. Hot-tempered, unconventional, and always willing to take the offensive, he became known as a raider for his risk taking, quick attacks on horseback, numerous close calls, and narrow escapes. His tactics were not learned from military textbooks but resembled Native American warfare in which men hid behind trees, used decoys, and clubbed the enemy with guns when ammunition ran low.

Forrest was never a man to give in without a struggle. When he was part of the Confederate force at Fort Donelson that was bottled up by Federals in February 1862, Forrest said to his men, "Boys, these people are talking about surrendering, and I am going out of this place before they do or bust hell wide open."[140] He and five hundred men escaped without a single shot being fired.

When Forrest was surrounded and seriously wounded while screening retreating Confederates at the Battle of Shiloh in April of that same year, he managed to escape by hoisting an unwary Federal onto his horse and using him as a shield while he raced out of range of the enemy. The legend of Forrest, "the Wizard of the Saddle," was born, and he gained renown for his remarkable ability to outmaneuver his enemies.

Western Operations

In late 1862, Forrest was assigned to cut Union general Ulysses S. Grant's supply lines in western Tennessee. According to historian Bruce Catton, he went "rampaging north along the Mobile & Ohio [Railroad], capturing Union supply and ammunition dumps, brushing off hostile patrols, seizing the horses, weapons, and other equipment he needed, and utterly

"Give Me the Point"

After countless engagements, seasoned veterans knew how best to survive against terrible odds. In *Reflections on the Civil War*, Pulitzer Prize–winning historian Bruce Catton recounts one of their scraps of wisdom, referencing seasoned cavalryman Nathan Bedford Forrest, whose weapons of choice were the saber and the pistol.

> The veteran cavalryman learned that the thing to do with a saber was not to hit the other man with it; it was to stick him with it. Unless you hit him in the face, slashing almost certainly wouldn't do any lasting damage. If you plunged the thing into him, you could end his life. In 1864 Confederate Bedford Forrest, who probably was the best cavalryman and one of the hardest fighters of the whole war, got into a fight. . . . He and a young Union officer struggled . . . and Forrest got the better of him. A few days later, he was talking to a Union officer who had come into camp under a flag of truce to deliver a message, and they got to talking about that fight. The officer asked him about it and Forrest said, "You know, if that young feller had had sense enough to give me the point, I wouldn't be here right now, but he tried to cut, which was his last mistake."

This Union officer is equipped with a rifle and a saber. The saber was best used to pierce, not cut, an opponent.

ruining the railroad for a stretch of sixty miles or more."[141]

When Grant sent men to stop him, Forrest's forces engaged the enemy near the tiny community of Parker's Cross-roads. In the midst of the engagement, the Confederates were unexpectedly hit from the rear by another party of Feder-als. As a panicky staff officer asked what they should do, Forrest said calmly and succinctly, "Split in two and charge both ways."[142] The Confederates did, and man-aged to battle their way to safety.

Although independent and unconven-tional, Forrest and his men allied themselves with the regular army at times. At the Battle of Chickamauga in September 1863, one of Forrest's fellow officers remarked, "[For-rest], though not of my command, most heartily cooperated throughout the day and rendered the most valuable service. I would ask no better fortune, if again placed on a flank, than to have such a vigilant, gallant, and accomplished officer guarding its ap-proaches."[143] Forrest was so angry with Gen-eral Braxton Bragg, who failed to follow up the Confederate victory at Chickamauga, however, that he threatened to kill him and transferred out of Bragg's command shortly thereafter.

Best and Worst

Despite his sometimes unorthodox ap-proach to fighting, Forrest was conven-tional when it came to discipline. A man who appreciated order and expected obe-dience, he demanded much from his men, and he could fly into a rage and punish them severely for insubordination or dere-liction of duty. For these qualities, he was appreciated and loved by some, feared and despised by others. One of the latter said, "'The Wizzard' now commands us . . . and I must express my distaste to being commanded by a man having no preten-sion to gentility. . . . [He] may be & no doubt is, the best Cav officer in the West, but I object to a tyrannical, hotheaded vul-garian's commanding me."[144]

Forrest *was* hotheaded, vulgar, and, because of his lack of education, barely able to read or write. Nevertheless, his leadership talents were appreciated by his superiors, and he was promoted to brigadier general in 1862 and to major general in December 1863. In February 1865, he was promoted to lieutenant gen-eral. From his beginnings as a private, his rise in rank was the greatest achievement of any man in either army during the war.

Despite such achievements, many Americans felt Forrest overstepped the bounds of humanity during his capture of Fort Pillow in Tennessee in April 1864. Originally a Confederate post, Fort Pillow was garrisoned by about six hundred Fed-erals, half of them blacks who had for-merly been slaves. When Forrest and his men captured the fort, almost 80 percent of the blacks were killed or wounded, a sign of the widespread rage felt by South-erners against blacks who dared oppose them. One Confederate wrote home, de-scribing how "the poor, deluded negroes would run up to our men, fall upon their knees and with uplifted hands scream for mercy, but were ordered to their feet and then shot down." [145]

Forrest did not take part in the killing, but he made little or no effort to stop it. The episode was reported in newspapers in the North, and the massacre at Fort Pillow became one of the outrages of the war.

"The Very Devil"

Forrest did not have the men or resources to make a difference in the final outcome of the war, but during the course of the four-year conflict, he built a reputation that endowed him with almost superhuman ability. Lee himself, when asked to name the greatest soldier produced on either side, reportedly stated, "A man I have never seen, sir. His name is Forrest." [146]

Part of Forrest's reputation was based on the Battle of Brices Cross Roads near Tupelo, Mississippi, on June 10, 1864. Forrest was confronted there by almost ten thousand Union soldiers sent to stop him from pursuing Union general William Tecumseh Sherman's army and cutting its supply lines. With only half the men that Sherman's army had, he first scattered the advance Federal cavalry force, then routed the infantry that followed, chasing them for miles until they all but dropped from exhaustion. "Forrest is the very devil," Sherman said in response to the defeat, and issued an order to "follow Forrest to the death if it costs 10,000 lives and breaks the Treasury.

There will never be peace in Tennessee till Forrest is dead." [147]

Defeat and Surrender

In the summer of 1864, Sherman began his campaign into the heart of the South, and in November of that year, Forrest was assigned to join forces with Confederate general John Bell Hood, whose mission was to pull Sherman out of Georgia by cutting his supply and communication lines in Tennessee. The effort proved a failure. Forrest did what he could to wreak havoc with the enemy, but by then his men were too tired, hungry, and weak to turn the war around single-handedly.

In January 1865, placed in charge of all cavalry forces in the department of Alabama, Mississippi, and east Louisiana, Forrest headed into Alabama, where the Federals were threatening the factories and foundries of Selma. There he fought his last battle on April 2 and was soundly defeated by Union general James H. Wilson. Seven days later, Robert E. Lee surrendered to Union general Ulysses S. Grant at Appomattox Court House, and the war came to an end.

Although Forrest considered escaping to Mexico rather than surrendering, he ultimately decided that he and his men could serve the South better if they returned to their homes. "Obey the laws, preserve your honor, and the government to which you have surrendered can afford to be and will be magnanimous," [148] he told them.

Grand Wizard Forrest

Forrest returned home to Memphis determined to become a planter again and restore his fortunes. Since he still retained property in the South, he succeeded to some extent, but he faced difficulties finding laborers and was accused of murdering one of the freedmen on his plantation. (He stood trial and was found not guilty.)

Unsettled postwar conditions across the South, particularly racial unrest and radical Republicans' attempts to reconstruct Southern society, soon motivated him to become involved in the Ku Klux Klan, one of several newly formed secret societies that aimed to ensure white supremacy through intimidation and violence. Although he denied all involvement, he was widely believed to be the grand wizard of the Klan for several years. As the organization grew, spread, and became extremely violent, however, Forrest relinquished his leadership. Historian Wyn C. Wade said, "When Grand Wizard Forrest realized that his so-called 'honorable and patriotic' organization had become a sprawling, intractable monster, he . . . wanted no further part of it."[149] Others believed Forrest resigned not because of escalat-

Two members of the Ku Klux Klan pose with their hoods and weapons. Forrest was believed to be the grand wizard of the Klan.

ing violence but because he could no longer control or regulate the Klan to suit his wishes.

Everlasting Controversy

Forrest remained outspoken and hot-tempered throughout his life, but he mellowed somewhat as time passed. "I have seen too much violence," he told a friend, "and I want to close my days at peace with all the world, as I am now at peace with my Maker."[150] The cavalryman died as a result of his many war wounds on October 29, 1877.

Forrest remains a controversial figure in history: Some see him as a symbol of racism, whereas others believe him to be a Southern hero, one of the greatest American cavalrymen of all time. Despite the divergence of opinion, all can agree that he was a rough and untutored product of the era in which he lived, one of the few Confederate military men who rose to fame solely through his own efforts and his own ability. Biographer Brian Steel Wills concludes, "Perhaps it is only fitting that Forrest continues to generate controversy, for he certainly did nothing to avoid it while he lived."[151]

Philip Sheridan

Less controversial but just as warlike as Nathan Bedford Forrest, Philip Sheridan was born on or about March 6, 1831, the third of six children in an Irish immigrant family. The location of his birth is as uncertain as his birthdate. He claimed to be a native of Albany, New York, but his mother stated that he was born aboard a ship en route from Ireland to America.

Sheridan was raised in Somerset, Ohio, and from his early years he was fascinated by the thought of battles and wars. In particular, the Mexican War of 1846 captured his imagination. "The stirring events of the times so much impressed and absorbed me that my sole wish was to become a soldier, and my highest aspirations to go to West Point as a cadet,"[152] he remembered. He got his wish in 1848, but the U.S. Military Academy was not exactly what he had imagined. He was a poor student, he was quarrelsome, and he accumulated many demerits for breaking the rules. At one point he was suspended for a year because of his hot temper.

Sheridan managed to graduate in 1853 and was assigned to an isolated post in southwestern Texas. As war loomed in early 1861, Sheridan benefited from the resignation of numerous men who sided with the Confederacy, and he was promoted to first lieutenant. Two months later he became a captain. He joked to a friend that if things continued on the same path, "perhaps I may . . . earn a major's commission."[153] In fact, his advances exceeded his wildest expectations. In September 1862 he was promoted to brigadier general of volunteers and, by war's end, had achieved the rank of major general in the regular army.

"Tornado in Battle"

During the war, Sheridan served for a time as chief quartermaster—the officer in charge of purchasing and distributing food, clothes, and other supplies to the

Hot-tempered, profane, and warlike, General Philip Sheridan earned a reputation as being a "tornado in battle" at Stones River.

army—in Missouri, then was assigned to a fighting unit in Tennessee. His reputation as a top-notch clerk followed him, however, and he was again put to work securing and transporting supplies rather than fighting Confederates. Such work was uninspiring to the impatient, diminutive warrior (he was just 5'5" and weighed less than 150 pounds), and he remained eager for an opportunity to escape clerking for fighting.

He got his chance unexpectedly in May 1862, when he was appointed colonel of the 2nd Regiment Michigan Cavalry stationed in northern Mississippi. Sheridan knew nothing of the cavalry, but he was a capable horseman and quickly fit in to his new regiment. Transferred to the infantry in late December 1862, he took part in the Battle of Stones River (Murfreesboro) in Tennessee, where he won a reputation as being a "perfect tornado in battle," both for his untiring energy and for his profanity. His commanding officer remembered, "He was pouring such a volume of oaths as made my blood curdle." [154]

Taking Missionary Ridge

In September 1863, Sheridan was part of the Union defeat at the Battle of Chickamauga, Tennessee, and in November of that same year, he helped recover that loss by his actions at the Battle of Chattanooga.

During that battle, without waiting for orders, Sheridan led an energetic charge up the craggy heights of Missionary Ridge, storming Confederate forces that were entrenched above the town. The slopes were so steep in some places that the Federals had to crawl and use tree branches to haul themselves upward, but they persevered and their forward momentum caused them to race past Confederate rifle pits and artillery when they reached easier terrain. "A column of Yankees swept right over where I was standing," one Confederate later wrote. "I was trying to stand aside to get out of their way, but the more I tried to get out of their way, the more in their way I got." [155]

By the end of their upward sweep that day, the Federals managed to capture more than three thousand prisoners and almost forty cannon. The jubilant Sheridan celebrated by jumping astride one of the big guns that sat on the mountain crest. He cheered and waved his hat as

Come Join the Cavalry

Many new recruits did not understand that life in the cavalry was extremely challenging and required commitment and hard work. In Davis, Pohanka, and Troiani's *Civil War Journal: The Leaders*, historians Edward G. Longacre and Brian Pohanka describe the arduous lifestyle of mounted forces in the Union army.

The popular conception of the cavalryman was that he was a kind of knight-errant . . . a soldier who would fight the war in a refined and exalted way. In 1861 that sort of image drew hordes of young men into the Union cavalry, but most of those recruits were not cavalry material.

Some joined the cavalry thinking that they would rather ride than walk from the beginning of the war to its conclusion. They quickly learned that the demands of the cavalry service were in many ways greater than that of the infantry. In the cavalry, the first thing each trooper did was to feed, water, and groom his horse. The infantry could loaf and socialize, but the cavalry worked constantly. In that division of the army, horses came first, men second. . . .

Horse soldiers first had to get acquainted with their animals and learn how to use them in battle. Second, they had to learn to fight in unison and formation. Pvt. Lucian P. Waters of the Eleventh New York Cavalry complained: "The cavalry tactics are ten times more difficult to learn than those of the infantry. The wheeling into columns and platoons are very difficult to thoroughly commit to memory."

the demoralized Confederates rushed wildly down the mountain and into the woods.

Led by Sheridan, Federal troops charge Missionary Ridge. The soldiers had to crawl and use tree limbs to haul themselves upward.

Strike Force

Sheridan's courageous actions at Chattanooga earned him the praise of his superior, General Ulysses S. Grant. When Grant was made general in chief of all Union armies in March 1864, he chose Sheridan to command the cavalry for the Army of the Potomac and directed him to convert his units into a strike force of significant power.

Unlike its Confederate counterpart, the Union cavalry had been used primarily to protect supply trains, to serve as messengers, and to ride guard around the edges of the encamped infantry in the early years of the war. Although it had been strengthened and reorganized, and had distinguished itself at the Battle of Brandy Station (the largest cavalry battle in North America) in June 1863, the cavalry was still subordinate to the main Federal army.

Sheridan determined to change all that. Enthusiastically, he spent the first month improving conditions for both men and horses, requesting additional supplies, and working out a plan by which the cavalry could be consolidated and used to the best effect against the enemy. At the same time, he set about gaining the support of the men he commanded, one of whom was dashing young general George Armstrong Custer.

Cavalrymen like Custer were inclined to look down on infantrymen, whom they derogatorily nicknamed "foot-sloggers." Then, too, Sheridan had served in the West, and Eastern soldiers tended to be skeptical of Westerners' abilities. Sheridan soon won their loyalty, however. Although he was volatile, vain, and sometimes inclined to shift blame to other men's shoulders, he was also brave and coolheaded in battle, and was often found at the head of a charge, unlike some other commanders. His men learned that they could trust him, even in difficult times. Historian Brian Pohanka points out, "By his voice and by his example, Sheridan had an amazing power of leadership over men in battle that made

them at least attempt to do the impossible."[156]

Thrashing Stuart

In May 1864, as Grant set out to do battle against Confederate general Robert E. Lee in the Wilderness of Virginia, Sheridan had his first chance to prove the value of his "new" cavalry. He proposed that he and his men be allowed to lead a strike against Jeb Stuart's renowned cavalry, claiming that he could "thrash hell out of Stuart any day."[157]

Sheridan's immediate superior, General George Meade, strongly disagreed. Prejudiced against the cavalry, he insisted that Sheridan and his men remain with the supply train they had been assigned to guard. Sheridan persisted in his demands, so Meade exasperatedly turned to his own superior, Grant, and repeated the boast. Laconic and practical, Grant replied, "Did Sheridan say that? Well, he generally knows what he is talking about. Let him start right out and do it."[158]

In the days that followed, Sheridan and his ten thousand men lured Stuart's cavalry away from the main Confederate army and across the Virginia countryside. The two mounted forces met at Yellow Tavern, a deserted inn ten miles north of Richmond, on May 11, 1864. There, in a heated battle, the Federals lived up to Sheridan's expectations by killing Stuart. Sheridan later stated, "Under him [Stuart], the cavalry of Lee's army . . . had acquired such prestige that it thought itself well nigh invincible. . . . This was now dispelled . . . and the removal of Stuart at Yellow Tavern had inflicted a blow from which entire recovery was impossible."[159]

"The Burning"

A proven combat force after Yellow Tavern, Sheridan's cavalry was given other important assignments. In July 1864, Grant sent them to the Shenandoah Valley, known as the "back door on Washington" since it lay just to the west of the capital city. Long held by Confederates, the valley presented a constant threat to the safety of the Federal capital. Confederate general Jubal A. Early and his fifteen thousand troops were the latest menace to Northern safety and peace of mind. In addition, guerrilla bands known as irregulars—soldiers and valley inhabitants—were always sniping at Union work parties, derailing supply trains, and keeping Federal soldiers on edge when they rode through the region.

To put an end to such harassment, Grant put Sheridan in charge of the Army of the Shenandoah, made up of cavalrymen and infantry troops. Although resistance was heavy, the general finally crushed Early's men in a sharp battle near Winchester in mid-September, the final blow coming from a division of Federal cavalry that swept around the Confederate flank, and sent them flying in confusion.

Then, with orders to make the valley a barren waste so that it could no longer support the enemy, Sheridan's army marched through the region in a campaign of looting and arson that came to be known as "The Burning." His men burned more than two thousand barns filled with grain and farm implements, destroyed seventy mills, and drove off more than four thousand head of cattle and horses and three thousand sheep. "The atmosphere, from horizon to horizon, has been black with the smoke of a hundred conflagrations,"[160] one man wrote.

The campaign was an example of total warfare waged against those who supported the Confederacy, and it effectively destroyed resistance in the Shenandoah Valley for the rest of the war. "As war is a punishment, if we can, by reducing its advocates to poverty, end it quicker, we are on the side of humanity,"[161] Sheridan stated.

Wrapping Up the War

In February 1865 Sheridan left the Shenandoah Valley and headed for Petersburg, Virginia, where Grant was bringing the war to an end. The fiery general was in the thick of the action at the Battle of Five Forks outside Petersburg on April 1, defeating General George Pickett and taking more than five thousand Confederate soldiers prisoner. Historian Paul A. Hutton points out the strengths of Sheridan's tactics at this time: "Sheridan . . . employed cavalry effectively as dismounted skirmishers. . . . He also used cavalry en masse, noting that ten thousand horsemen crashing into an enemy line could bring about

Dead horses and ruined wagons were just some of the results of Sheridan's march through the Shenandoah Valley.

enormous confusion and create opportunities for the infantry."[162]

When Lee fled from Petersburg, Sheridan continued his harassment of the Confederates, capturing their few remaining supply trains and pressuring them to the point of exhaustion. "I am still pressing on with both cavalry and infantry," he told Grant on April 6. "If the thing is pressed I think Lee will surrender."[163]

It was Sheridan's cavalry plus a corps of infantry that squarely blocked Lee's road on April 9 as the Confederates tried one final escape. Sheridan was preparing for a fresh attack when a messenger arrived with the news, "Lee has surrendered; do not charge;

the white flag is up." Sheridan held up a clenched fist in victory. "I've got 'em like that!"[164] he shouted.

Not one to miss the conclusion of a great event, Sheridan made sure he was at the surrender ceremony that took place that afternoon in a private home at Appomattox Court House, Virginia. He even managed to spirit away a few souvenirs such as the small table on which Grant composed the surrender terms.

Final Challenges

After the war ended, Sheridan was appointed military governor of Texas and Louisiana during the period of reorganization and rebuilding known as Reconstruction. In mid-1867 the severity of his administration caused President Andrew Johnson to transfer him to the Department of the Missouri, where he spent the next fifteen years fighting Native Americans, pausing in 1875 to get married for the first time.

In 1884, Sheridan became commanding general of the U.S. Army. Just prior to his death, Congress voted to make him a full general, a rank that had been awarded only to Sherman and Grant. Sheridan died of a heart attack on August 5, 1888.

Although disliked by many and condemned by some as a braggart and a showoff, Sheridan was highly valued by those who knew him best. Many historians believe that the Union cavalry could not have achieved its great success without him, because he was able to inspire his men to attempt—and accomplish—valorous deeds. Despite his shortcomings, Philip Sheridan's contributions to the war will never be overlooked, just as his bold, forceful authority will never be forgotten.

☆ Chapter 6 ☆

Women of Courage

Women could not take official leadership roles during the Civil War because society saw them as weak and emotional creatures, capable of little more than housekeeping and childbearing. Despite such social restrictions, however, women managed to serve their country in a variety of ways outside the home. Some were camp cooks and laundresses, others volunteered to be nurses. In the North, some women were members of the Sanitary Commission, a relief agency that distributed everything from onions to underwear to men in the camps.

A few women were true leaders who single-handedly fought opposition and braved public opinion to serve in a manner of their own choosing. Clara Barton and Mary Edwards Walker were two such individuals. Author Elizabeth D. Leonard writes, "[They] refused to accept the idea that war was 'no place for women.' Instead they . . . declared themselves, like men, citizens and patriots who had a right to participate actively in the Union's defense." [165]

Clara Barton

Clarissa Harlowe Barton was born on Christmas Day in 1821 on a prosperous farm near Oxford, Massachusetts. Nicknamed Clara, the little girl was intelligent but small and plain, and she suffered from a minor speech impediment. All these factors combined to intensify her sensitivity and self-consciousness. "The sensitive nature will always remain," [166] opined a visitor to the Barton home. He recommended work to help the timid, introspective young girl gain confidence.

"The Hide of a Shark"

Clara became a schoolteacher at about the age of eighteen and, according to her cousin, was a fine and natural educator. Because of discrimination in the workplace, she left the schoolroom at the age

Before becoming a nurse, Clara Barton had been a schoolteacher and a clerk. Discrimination toughened her resolve.

patent applications and other documents, she again faced discrimination from her male colleagues, but this time she managed to cope with it. "It wasn't a pleasant experience," she conceded, "in fact, it was very trying, but I thought perhaps there was some question of principle involved and I lived it through."[167]

In fact, working for months with men who tried to drive her off the job helped toughen her resolve. "Any blow that they could slanderously aim at me in *these* days, would make about as much impression upon me [as] a sling shot would upon the hide of a Shark—I have got above them,"[168] she told a friend.

Barton was working at the Patent Office when war broke out in 1861. She instantly decided to volunteer to care for the wounded but soon realized that the soldiers who gathered in Washington had other needs that no one was addressing. Many had neglected to pack necessities such as paper and pencils, needles and thread, soap and towels. Intently, Barton set out to do what she could to gather and distribute supplies to them, using her own money to purchase as many goods as she could afford. When her funds ran short, she wrote letters to friends, acquaintances, and clergymen, who willingly assumed re-

of thirty-two, however, and entered the second phase of her career, becoming the first female clerk in the U.S. Patent Office in Washington, D.C. There, while copying

sponsibility for gathering the many tons of blankets, canned food, clothes, and medical supplies that Barton eventually distributed in the camps.

Fight for Acceptance

As the war progressed and the Army of the Potomac saw action at Bull Run (Manassas) in July 1861, Barton's focus expanded. She learned that lives were needlessly lost simply because there was not enough help on the battlefield. Some men lay where they fell for three or four days after an engagement, and even those who were carried to safety sometimes did not receive treatment because medical supplies ran short.

Barton determinedly wrote to officials in the War Department and asked permission to carry medicines, bandages, and other supplies to the battle zone, even though the presence of an unattended woman among so many men was considered highly improper at the time. Most officials whom she petitioned refused, convinced that a woman would "skeedaddle and create a panic,"[169] when danger threatened.

Because there was not enough help on the battlefield, many men wounded in combat lay where they fell for days.

Although she was frustrated, Barton persevered and finally gained the attention of Colonel Daniel H. Rucker in the quartermaster's office, the department responsible for feeding, clothing, and equipping troops. When Rucker learned that the small, plainly dressed woman before him had three warehouses of hospital supplies and food ready to be conveyed to his army in the field, he instantly gave her the pass she had been demanding. From then on, Barton was unstoppable. Her desire to serve overcame her modesty and her natural fears, and she followed the army wherever it went for the next four years.

"Homely Angel"

Conscientious enough to deliver her supplies personally, Barton quickly discovered that, to be of greatest help to surgeons and troops in the field, she and her wagonloads of supplies needed to be some of the first to arrive at a battle scene. Guided by gunfire, she would hurry to position herself where she was most needed. One harassed surgeon, working to save the wounded after the Battle of Cedar Mountain in August 1861, stated, "I thought that night if heaven ever sent out a homely angel, she must be one, her assistance was so timely."[170]

Once at her destination, Barton would kindle fires, prepare hot soup, and unwrap bandages and dressings that she would use to staunch wounds. When supplies ran out, she improvised. One morning she made breakfast for hungry troops using crushed army biscuits, wine, water, and brown sugar, serving it in empty jelly jars and wine bottles. "Not very inviting you will think, but I assure you always acceptable,"[171] she stated. When bureaucratic red tape got in her way, she ruthlessly cut it and went on. For instance, after one battle near Fredericksburg, Barton discovered that military officials had not asked wealthy citizens of the town to open their homes or share their hidden supplies of food with "her men" who lay wounded, cold, and hungry on the floors of hotels and other public buildings. Barton hurried to Washington, demanded immediate action from the War Department, and succeeded in obtaining both food and lodging for those in need.

"My Own Army"

Barton did more than procure supplies, however. She also served as a nurse, and unlike most other women nurses, who stayed behind the lines and in city hospitals, she went directly onto the battlefield to do her nursing. Her face gray from gunpowder, her skirts heavy with blood, she quickly adjusted to the horrific sights and smells that were common in field hospitals, and she grew adept at helping with surgeries, bandaging wounds, and easing the suffering and dying of thousands of men. One time she removed a bullet from an injured man's jaw; another time she was almost killed while offering

The Misery of War

After the staggering Union defeat at the Battle of Fredericksburg in December 1862, Clara Barton and other relief workers set up several temporary hospitals in the area to care for thousands of wounded Federal soldiers. One of those hospitals was Lacy House, an elegant eighteenth-century mansion set in the village of Falmouth. Conditions there are described in Elizabeth Brown Pryor's *Clara Barton: Professional Angel.*

Barton was everywhere in that pinched and unhappy town, saw every wretched collection of wounded men, knew every ugly corner. What stayed in her memory, though, was the dreadful confusion of the Lacy House. Clara did not flinch, as did fellow worker Walt Whitman, at the pile of amputated arms, legs, and feet that graced the door of the mansion—she had seen them piled to the shoulders of operating surgeons during the heat of battle. But even a soul as inured as hers gasped at the spectacle of hundreds of sufferers crammed onto floors slippery with blood, balanced on the shelves of china cupboards, and wedged under the legs of tables. The agony there . . . seemed so immense that she later estimated that twelve hundred men were at the Lacy House. . . .

Individual names and faces from the house came back to Barton over the years:—a man saved by a tourniquet repeatedly saying as he clutched at her skirt, "You saved my life"; an officer, fatally shot, believing in his delirium that she was his wife. Recalling to a friend the terrors of this place, Barton remarked that when she rose from the side of one soldier, "I wrung the blood from the bottom of my clothing, before I could step, for the weight about my feet." For her the Lacy House became synonymous with inefficiency, needless suffering, and all the collected misery of the war.

a man a drink of water. "A bullet sped its full and easy way between us, tearing a hole in my sleeve and found its way into his body,"[172] she remembered. The man died in her arms.

Barton was an independent woman who felt confined and unhappy when she was among other relief workers. She came to see the Army of the Potomac as "my own army," dedicating herself to caring for its wounded throughout the entire war. Although she grew battle-hardened, she was still horrified by the numbers of men killed and wounded during Union general Ulysses S. Grant's campaign to destroy Lee's army in 1864. "I am holding my breath in awe at the vastness of the shadow that floats like a pall over our head," she told a friend. "It has come that man has no longer an individual existence but is counted in thousands and measured in miles."[173]

"Plod on Day by Day"

While Grant and Lee squared off in months of fighting from the Virginia Wilderness to Spotsylvania and Cold Harbor, Barton labored tirelessly at the crowded Fredericksburg hospitals, where most wounded soldiers from the Army of the Potomac were treated. Eventually, she was overtaken by exhaustion. "I have had

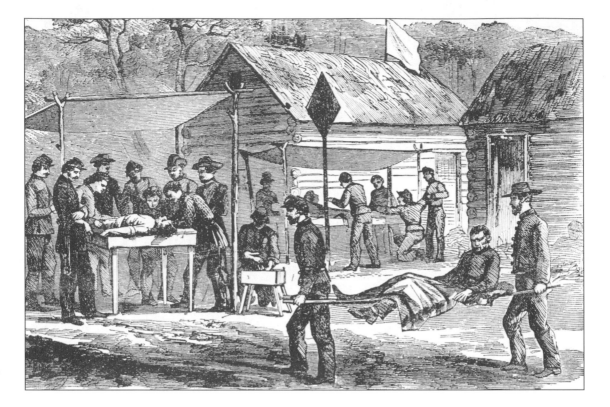

Wounded men are brought to a makeshift Union corps hospital after a battle. Barton worked in similar surroundings in order to remain close to the fighting.

but one night's sleep since last Thursday," she wrote on a Tuesday in late May 1864. "I had so many personal friends that were mortally wounded, and just reached our city to die—we are waiting at the cotside and closing their eyes one by one as they pass away."[174]

By June 1864, Grant had besieged Lee at Petersburg, a railroad center near the Confederate capital of Richmond, and Barton had accepted a less stressful position at a corps hospital in the vicinity. There she served as a cook, nurse, and director of the nursing staff.

As the war entered its last months, the hospital was repeatedly moved closer to the fighting, and Barton was faced with the grueling tasks of packing and unpacking supplies, finding new quarters, and ensuring that her patients were carefully tended. "I cannot tell you how many times I have moved with my whole family of a thousand or fifteen hundred and with a half hour's notice in the night," she wrote. "I do not bother my poor head about the end but plod on day by day, trying to perform my round of duty faithfully."[175]

New Endeavor

Barton's duties as supply agent and nurse came to a close when the war ended on April 9, 1865. Always happiest when she was busy, she immediately began a new endeavor—working to determine the fate of soldiers who were missing at war's end. Well known for her compassion and accomplishments, she had received innumerable letters from families during the war asking if she had nursed their loved ones or knew of their fate. In her efforts to provide answers, she learned that more than half of the Federal soldiers who had been killed in battle remained unidentified, and almost 200,000 graves marked "Unknown" were scattered across the country.

To expedite her undertaking, Barton set up an "Office of Correspondence with Friends of the Missing Men of the U.S. Army" at Annapolis, Maryland. She also published lists of missing men, organized by state, in newspapers and post offices throughout the nation, hoping that other veterans would read them and give her information. "I am oh so busy," she wrote to a friend. "My plan is a perfect success and is growing popular I think—at least no one condemns it that I know of." [176]

One day she was visited by a soldier who had been a prisoner at the infamous Confederate prison camp Andersonville. He had surreptitiously kept a list of thirteen hundred of the men who died there, and Barton was able to notify their families of their deaths. Barton continued her work for three years and helped locate over twenty-two thousand men. Never strong, however, her health broke in 1868, and she went abroad to rest, recuperate, and begin a new chapter in her unique career.

American Red Cross

In the summer of 1870, war broke out between France and Prussia (present-day northern Germany and Poland). Still in Europe at the time, Barton volunteered her services to a new relief organization, the Red Cross, which had been founded in Switzerland in about 1863. Impressed by its achievements, she later lobbied the U.S. government to allow a branch to be established in America. The struggle was longer than any she had endured in the Civil War, but she persevered, and in 1881, the first chapter of the American National Red Cross (soon renamed the American Red Cross) was established in Dansville, New York.

Other chapters soon followed, and the relief organization eventually earned an impressive reputation by aiding victims of fire, flood, and other disasters throughout the United States. Barton served as its first president until 1904, when she was eighty-two years old.

"A Woman's Power"

In addition to her relief work, Clara Barton allied herself with the women's rights movement during the latter half of her life, lecturing and speaking out on such topics as women's equality, equal education opportunities, fair pay, and the right to vote.

She often referred to the difficulties she had encountered carrying out her relief work. "Mine has not been the kind of work usually given to women to perform," she explained, "and no man *can* quite comprehend the situation. No man is ever called to do a man's work with only a woman's power and surroundings."[177]

Barton spent the last years of her life living in Glen Echo, Maryland, writing, gardening, and carrying out such humble chores as painting her house and milking cows. All the while she wore the many medals she had been awarded for her life of service, among them the International Red Cross Medal, the Iron Cross of Imperial Germany, and the Cross of Imperial Russia. She died of pneumonia on April 12, 1912, at the age of ninety.

Barton is remembered as a great humanitarian and a role model for women. She is an example of what one person can accomplish despite personal insecurity and the restrictiveness of society. Clara Barton remains, as one contemporary expressed, a "true heroine of the age, the angel of the battlefield."[178]

Mary Edwards Walker

The only female surgeon to serve in the Civil War, Mary Edwards Walker was born on November 26, 1832, in Oswego, New York, to a reform-minded couple who encouraged their daughter to develop her intellect while learning the value of hard work on the family farm. Influenced by their example, Mary made a career choice based on logic rather than convention. She decided

Mary Edwards Walker was the only female surgeon to serve during the Civil War. She courageously pursued her dream of becoming an army doctor.

to become a doctor, and at the age of twenty, she entered Syracuse Medical College in New York State, one of the nation's first medical schools to accept both men and women on an equal basis.

Although it was a fine institution, some practitioners did not recognize Syracuse as a true medical school because it emphasized dietary, herbal, and water therapies as alternatives to more accepted practices of the time, such as bloodletting, blistering, and large doses of medication. Throughout the war, Walker's medical competence was challenged not only because of her sex but because of her alma mater.

Brazen and Shameless

Walker also faced opposition because of her choice of clothing. Her parents had taught her that tight-fitting garments such as corsets were unhealthy. As she grew up, Walker not only remembered their teachings, but she took them one step further. She became convinced that conventional women's clothing—long dresses and petticoats that were tight, multilayered, cumbersome, and inclined to collect dirt—endangered a woman's health and sanity. "The greatest sorrows from which women suffer today are those physical, moral, and mental ones, that are caused by their unhygienic manner of dressing,"[179] she wrote in 1871.

Practicing what she preached, Walker chose to wear more practical attire—a one-piece garment that served as underwear, loose trousers with suspenders, and a knee-length dress with a waist, long sleeves, high neck, and full skirt. Although extremely modest by today's standards, such clothing—particularly the trousers—shocked and outraged many of her contemporaries, who saw her as brazen, shameless, and immoral.

Female Doctor

Walker graduated from Syracuse in 1855 and married a fellow medical student named Albert Miller. She wore bloomers (wide, loose pants) to the wedding, omitted the word *obey* from her vows, and retained her maiden name. Albert proved unfaithful, however, and the marriage did not last. When the Civil War began in 1861, Walker moved to Washington, D.C., to seek an official commission as a surgeon in the U.S. Army. Her actions offended most men she petitioned. Female nurses were gradually becoming accepted, but female doctors were not. The army's growing determination to enlist doctors solely from recognized medical schools also worked against Walker's chances of success.

Deeply patriotic and determined to contribute her talents to the war effort, Walker gained permission to work as an assistant physician and surgeon in November 1861 in the Indiana Hospital, a temporary facility in Washington, D.C. The hospital's supervisor had recently lost his assistant and desperately needed help. "I need and desire her assistance here very much, believing as I do that she is well qualified for the

Walker served as a physician and surgeon at a temporary hospital much like this one. She often worked long hours without pay.

position. She is a graduate of a regular (sic) Medical College, and has had a number of years' extensive experience, and comes highly recommended,"[180] he wrote to Surgeon General Clement A. Finley.

Walker worked at Indiana Hospital about two months, diagnosing and treating illnesses, assisting in operations, prescribing medicine, and making a variety of other contributions to the war effort. Her dedication was so great that she served without pay, ate and slept at the hospital, and absorbed other personal expenses despite the fact that she had no other income at the time.

In the Field

In the fall of 1862, Walker offered her services to the Army of the Potomac, whose soldiers were suffering from a typhoid epidemic. In December, she traveled to Fredericksburg, Virginia, in the wake of Union general Ambrose Burnside's devastating defeat there. She helped care for the thousands of battered men who survived the battle and became hardened to the rough-and-ready emergency procedures that were being practiced by battlefield surgeons.

During her time in the field, Walker continued to serve selflessly, receiving no compensation for her work except for food, a tent, and the conviction that she

Pointed Advice

Mary Edwards Walker was horrified by the endless amputations that were performed during the war. As a student at Syracuse Medical School, she had learned less radical methods that were often equally effective. Realizing that if she, as a female, protested against conventional medical wisdom she could be removed from service, she contented herself with informing soldiers of their right to refuse such treatment. Her advice is included in Elizabeth D. Leonard's *Yankee Women*.

Whenever I found that there were contemplated operations, and a complaint from a soldier that a decision had been made to remove a limb, I casually asked to see it, and in almost every instance I saw amputation was not only unnecessary, but to me it seemed wickedly cruel. I would then swear the soldier not to repeat anything that I told him, and then I would tell him that no one was obliged to submit to an amputation unless he chose to do so, that his limbs belonged to himself. I then instructed him to protest against amputation, and that if the physicians insisted upon it that if he had never used a swearing word to swear and declare that if they forced him to have an operation that he would never rest after his recovery until he had shot them dead. I need not say that se-

crecy regarding what I had told to the soldier was kept and that my advice was followed and that many a man today has for it the perfect and good use of his limbs who would not have had but for my advice.

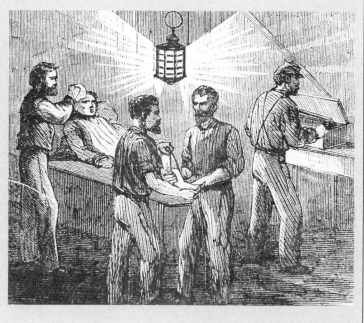

Surgeons prepare to amputate a foot. Mary Edwards Walker informed soldiers of their right to refuse such treatment.

was using her skills to good purpose. (At this time, surgeons in the army were usually paid between $100 and $169 per month, while army nurses earned about $12 per month.) One doctor with whom Walker worked discovered that she was working for no pay and wrote to Secretary of War Edwin M. Stanton, pointing out the injustice. Stanton replied that there could be no payment because "there is no authority of law for making allowance to you."[181]

Persistent Petitioner

After Fredericksburg, Walker returned to Washington, still hopeful of obtaining a commission but interested in doing other war-related work as well. Familiar with the problem of locating an inexpensive room when one was a respectable, single woman in Washington, she contacted a women's suffrage group and convinced them to establish a lodging house for some of the hundreds who came to the city in search of loved ones. The idea proved so popular that a second residence opened a short time later.

Walker also set up an information service to help women find missing relatives in the city. And when the soldiers she treated turned to her with their questions or problems, Walker served as a go-between for them and the military. One captain stated, "[My men] need mittens, and I know of no one except you on whom to make [this request] and expect it to be filled."[182]

Time was passing, and a commission still seemed out of reach for Walker in November 1863. Persistent and resourceful, however, she developed a new plan and wrote to Secretary of War Stanton with her proposal. "Will you give me authority to get up a regiment of men, to be called *Walker's U.S. Patriots*, subject to all general orders? . . . I would like the authority to enlist them in any loyal states, & also authority to tell them that I will act as first Assistant Surgeon."[183]

Stanton turned down her request. Undaunted, she turned to the president, but Lincoln also disappointed her with a refusal, claiming that "it would injure the [Medical Department] for me, with strong hand, to thrust among them anyone, male or female, against their consent."[184]

Contract Surgeon

Not sitting idly by while she waited for a reply from the War Department, Walker traveled to Tennessee in the fall of 1863, intent upon aiding the thousands of Federals who had been wounded in the Battle of Chickamauga, a bloody Union defeat that took place on September 19 and 20. The military physician in charge restricted her work to nursing, but her contributions earned her the respect of General George H. Thomas, head of the Army of the Cumberland. In January of the next year, Thomas sponsored her appointment as a civilian contract surgeon.

Happy to be officially allied with the army, Walker did her best to aid Thomas's

Walker's contributions to the treating of those wounded at the Battle of Chickamauga (pictured) earned her a promotion to civilian contract surgeon.

troops in Tennessee, although they were in winter quarters and would not be going into battle until spring. When not working in the camp, Walker reached out to civilians in the region, treating fevers, pulling teeth, and delivering babies. "The people . . . were in a pitiable condition," she wrote. "Both armies had been upon the ground . . . but the Confederate army had been all through there pressing every man into service."[185]

As a civilian and a physician, Walker was relatively free to move about the country-side. Some believed she served as an unofficial Union spy during this period. Whether she did or not, one day in April 1864, she wandered too far afield and was captured by Confederates who failed to believe the story she told of delivering letters. She was ques-

tioned, then taken across country to be imprisoned for four months at Castle Thunder Prison (a converted tobacco warehouse) in Richmond, Virginia. The reaction of one Confederate captain, present at the time of her arrest, reveals that the male bias against unorthodox females was not restricted to the North.

This morning we were all amused and disgusted too at the sight of a *thing* that nothing but the debased and the depraved Yankee nation could produce—

"a female doctor.". . . She was dressed in the full uniform of a Federal Surgeon, boots hat & all, & wore a cloak. . . . I was in hopes that General [Joseph E.] Johnston would have had her dressed in a homespun frock and bonnet and sent back to the Yankee lines, or put in a lunatic asylum.[186]

Shortly after her release from prison in August, Walker was assigned to be head surgeon at the Louisville Female Military Prison in Kentucky; she had been recommended by General George Thomas and his superior, General William Tecumseh Sherman, who had also been impressed by her qualifications and dedication. At the same time, she was awarded back pay and a salary of $100 per month.

Being head surgeon led many to believe that Walker had been commissioned in the army—she was often addressed as Major Dr. Walker—but she was not commissioned and remained a civilian contract surgeon. She battled constant harassment at Louisville, and her determination to end familiarity between guards and prisoners and to forbid disloyal talk among inmates (most of whom were Confederate spies and other disloyal females) earned her the dislike of many of the women prisoners who, ironically, refused to be treated by a female doctor.

Highest Honor

Dissatisfied with her assignment at Louisville, in March 1865 Walker requested transfer to the front as a surgeon. The war ended on April 9, 1865, however, frustrating her efforts. Nevertheless she continued to pursue a commission as a peacetime military surgeon, even writing to President Andrew Johnson and convincing numerous supporters to submit recommendations on her behalf.

To his credit, Johnson considered her request carefully. "It would seem . . . that she has performed service deserving the recognition of the Govt.—which I desire to give—if there is any way in which—or precedent by which this may be done,"[187] he wrote.

Despite Johnson's support, Walker's request was again denied, ostensibly because there was no law or precedent to authorize it. In fact, she was a woman in a time when few women pursued careers, and even fewer tried to enter male-dominated fields such as medicine. Johnson was so impressed by her credentials and her contributions to the war effort, however, that on November 11, 1865, he presented her with the Congressional Medal of Honor for Meritorious Service.

No Ordinary Woman

Mary Walker spent the years after the war working as a physician as well as a social reformist, particularly in the area of women's rights. She also filled her time writing and lecturing on such topics as dress reform and women's suffrage. She remained unpopular with many who saw her as too radical and who resented her strong challenge to traditional women's roles. To her satisfaction, she lived long enough to see women wearing trousers

Women and the Vote

Mary Walker wrote extensively during her lifetime and published *Hit*, a combination biography and commentary, in 1871. Although not a literary masterpiece, the following excerpt from the book reveals the author to be one of a handful of women of the age who outspokenly supported women's rights and equality for all.

> God has given to woman . . . important rights of individuality, as He has to man; and any manmade laws that deprive her of any rights or privileges, that are enjoyed by himself, are usurpations of power. Such laws are an outrage, and as much a contravention of God's laws, as though man deprived woman of her life; for her aspirations and freedom of soul, are as dear to her as is her life.
>
> Deity intended a free and full development of all of woman's powers, as well as man's, and gave her a mind to decide for herself in all things. There are thousands of cases on every hand, where more wretchedness, aye, *agony*, would be prevented by man's taking woman's *life* from her, than taking liberties that the Franchise [right to vote] would secure to her. . . .
>
> Man not having been deprived of his individuality, does not know the feeling of degradation, that woman experiences, and how her soul writhes under the chains that have inscribed upon them "thus far and no farther," *because you are a woman*. Why should there be anything said about what shall be the bounds of a woman's abilities, or where shall be the limits, any more than those of a man? He is free to make of himself what he is capable of doing, and no one is expected to interfere in his plans, *because he is a man enfranchised*.

and serving in the U.S. Army in World War I.

Although Walker's medal and those of nine hundred other individuals were revoked by the War Department in 1917 when Congress revised the standards under which they had been awarded, Mary Walker proudly continued to wear her decoration until her death in 1919. In 1977 President Jimmy Carter reinstated her award posthumously, and she remains the first and only woman to achieve that honor.

Walker remains a little-known but bona fide leader and role model for women in the Civil War. In the words of historian Elizabeth D. Leonard, this female physician and others like her, "by virtue of their own determination and courage, brought forth positive changes in popular characterizations of middle-class womanhood that, in turn, opened new doors for women in the professions and in public life."[188]

Chapter 7

Out of Many, One

After four years of bloodshed and millions of lost lives, the Civil War came to an end on April 9, 1865, when Robert E. Lee surrendered to Ulysses S. Grant at the tiny crossroads settlement of Appomattox Court House, Virginia. By then, the South was beaten and demoralized; its cities burned, its countryside laid waste, its economy in ruins. Although a formal peace was declared, decades would pass before the nation would come together in spirit, before the physical and emotional scars left by the conflict would fade.

Leaders of the conflict—those who had survived—were scarred as well. Like all who participated, they had endured sorrow, pain, and loss. All could claim the satisfaction of knowing that they had fought for the cause in which they believed, but many came out of the conflict with little else to show for the struggle. Still, they could look with pride on their years of service and say, in the words of William T. Sherman, "[We] have done all that men could do . . . and we have a right to join in the universal joy that fills our land because the war is *over*." [189]

Unparalleled Accomplishments

The Civil War was a tragic episode in U.S. history, a time when men expressed their views with bullets rather than ballots. Much came out of the tragedy, however, that was positive. There were contributions in the military—new and more efficient weaponry and new strategies for fighting—that would be used in later struggles against aggression and brutality. Relief and humanitarian efforts were taken to new heights. Women's rights were advanced as large numbers of "the weaker sex" proved capable of taking on tasks that had long been reserved for men.

Rebellion was suppressed, and the Union was restored. Democracy was proven to work despite terrible challenges to its endurance. The nation sur-

Union troops march through Washington, D.C., after the conclusion of the Civil War. The Union was restored.

vived its fiery trial and became a symbol of freedom and equality for others to emulate in the future.

America became a nation in the truc sense of the word. People no longer considered the country to be a loose collection of states that could be broken apart at will. Before the war, many Americans said, "The United States are . . . " After the war, the phrase became "The United States is . . . ,"[190] and the nation's motto, *E Pluribus Unum*, "out of many, one," took on new meaning for all time.

Slavery was abolished. In the words of William Lloyd Garrison, "The insubstantial dream of evil overthrown has become the fabric of reality."[191] Although many inequities and injustices remained to be addressed, the country had taken the first step in recognizing that *all* human beings deserve equal treatment under the law. Author and historian Bruce Catton writes,

The country made a commitment during that war; a commitment to a broader freedom, a broader citizenship. We [could] no longer be content

The Incommunicable Experience of War

Aside from the nation's leaders, many Americans attempted to express feelings inspired by the close of the nation's great cataclysm. Geoffrey C. Ward includes the thoughts of some who were ordinary and some more notable in his work *The Civil War: An Illustrated History.*

"Thank God it is over and that the Union is restored. And so at last I am a simple citizen. Well, I am content, but should my country call again I am ready to respond."

—Colonel Elisha Hunt Rhodes, Second Rhode Island Volunteers

"My shoes are gone; my clothes are almost gone. I'm weary, I'm sick, I'm hungry. My family have been killed or scattered. . . . And I have suffered all this for my country. I love my country. But if this war is ever over, I'll be damned if I ever love another country."

—Confederate soldier during the retreat to Appomattox

"Strange, (is it not?) that battles, martyrs, blood, even assassination should so condense—perhaps only really, lastingly condense—a Nationality."

—Walt Whitman, poet

"We have shared the incommunicable experience of war. We have felt, we still feel, the passion of life to its top. . . . In our youths, our hearts were touched by fire."

—Oliver Wendell Holmes Jr., writer

"The pageant has passed. The day is over. But we linger, loath to think we shall see them no more together—these men, these horses, these colors afield."

—General Joshua Lawrence Chamberlain, Twentieth Maine Infantry

with anything less than complete liberty, complete equality before law for all of our people regardless of their color, their race, their religion, their national origin; regardless of anything.[192]

"A Just and a Lasting Peace"

The Civil War was an epic event in American history, and few of America's leaders foresaw the price that would be paid to end the conflict. They did not know in the beginning the direction that the war would lead them. Still, most had dreamed of a meaningful peace, and that had been achieved.

Their best and highest aspirations for what was to follow were expressed by Abraham Lincoln before he died.

With malice toward none; with charity for all; with firmness in the right, as God gives us to see the right, let us strive on to finish the work we are in; to bind up the nation's wounds; to care for him who shall have borne the battle . . . to do all which may achieve and cherish a just and a lasting peace.[193]

★ Notes ★

Introduction: A National Perspective

1. Quoted in Geoffrey C. Ward, *The Civil War: An Illustrated History.* New York: Knopf, 1990, p. xvi.
2. Quoted in Shelby Foote, *The Civil War: A Narrative.* 3 vols. New York: Random House, 1958–1974, vol. 1, p. 39.
3. Quoted in Foote, *The Civil War,* vol. 1, p. 32.
4. Quoted in Ward, *The Civil War,* p. 166.
5. Quoted in Bruce Catton, *This Hallowed Ground.* Garden City, NY: Doubleday, 1956, p. 394.

Chapter 1: The Statesmen

6. Burton J. Hendrick, *Statesmen of the Lost Cause.* New York: Literary Guild of America, 1939, p. 21.
7. Quoted in William C. Davis, Brian C. Pohanka, and Don Troiani, eds., *Civil War Journal: The Leaders.* Nashville: Rutledge Hill Press, 1997, p. 68.
8. Quoted in Davis, Pohanka, and Troiani, *Civil War Journal,* p. 53.
9. Jefferson Davis, *Rise and Fall of the Confederate Government.* 2 vols. New York: D. Appleton, 1881, vol. 1, p. 230.
10. Quoted in Hendrick, *Statesmen of the Lost Cause,* p. 93.
11. Quoted in William C. Davis, *Jefferson Davis: The Man and His Hour.* New York: HarperCollins, 1991, p. 355.
12. Foote, *The Civil War,* vol. 1, p. 124.
13. Quoted in Davis, *Jefferson Davis,* p. 383.
14. Quoted in Davis, *Jefferson Davis,* p. 354.
15. Quoted in Davis, *Jefferson Davis,* p. 448.
16. Quoted in Davis, *Jefferson Davis,* p. 429.
17. Quoted in Foote, *The Civil War,* vol. 1, pp. 394, 395.
18. Quoted in Foote, *The Civil War,* vol. 3, p. 860.
19. Quoted in Davis, *Jefferson Davis,* p. 608.
20. Quoted in Foote, *The Civil War,* vol. 1, p. 21.
21. Quoted in Foote, *The Civil War,* vol. 1, p. 23.
22. Quoted in Foote, *The Civil War,* vol. 1, p. 27.
23. Quoted in Foote, *The Civil War,* vol. 1, pp. 39, 40.
24. Quoted in Foote, *The Civil War,* vol. 1, p. 30.
25. Quoted in Foote, *The Civil War,* vol. 1, p. 708.
26. Quoted in Foote, *The Civil War,* vol. 2, p. 833.
27. Quoted in Foote, *The Civil War,* vol. 1, p. 143.

28. Quoted in Foote, *The Civil War,* vol. 3, pp. 625–26.

29. Quoted in Foote, *The Civil War,* vol. 3, p. 986.

30. Frederick Douglass, *Autobiographies.* New York: Library of America, 1994, pp. 921, 924.

Chapter 2: The Abolitionists

31. Quoted in Walter M. Merrill, *Against Wind and Tide.* Cambridge, MA: Harvard University Press, 1963, p. 7.

32. Quoted in Merrill, *Against Wind and Tide,* p. 39.

33. Merrill, *Against Wind and Tide,* p. 45.

34. Quoted in Merrill, *Against Wind and Tide,* p. 45.

35. Quoted in Boston African American National Historic Site Biographies, "William Lloyd Garrison," taken from William S. Parsons and Margaret A. Drew, *The African Meeting House in Boston: A Sourcebook.* (n.p., n.d.). www.nps.gov/boaf/garris~1.htm.

36. Boston African American National Historic Site Biographies, "William Lloyd Garrison."

37. Quoted in Merrill, *Against Wind and Tide,* p. 201.

38. Quoted in Merrill, *Against Wind and Tide,* pp. 205, 214.

39. Quoted in Merrill, *Against Wind and Tide,* p. 272.

40. Quoted in Merrill, *Against Wind and Tide,* p. 276.

41. Quoted in Merrill, *Against Wind and Tide,* p. 275.

42. Quoted in Merrill, *Against Wind and Tide,* pp. 283, 292.

43. Quoted in Merrill, *Against Wind and Tide,* p. 300.

44. Quoted in Merrill, *Against Wind and Tide,* p. 330.

45. Boston African American National Historic Site Biographies, "William Lloyd Garrison."

46. Douglass, *Autobiographies,* p. 38.

47. Quoted in Davis, Pohanka, and Troiani, *Civil War Journal,* p. 166.

48. Douglass, *Autobiographies,* p. 350.

49. Quoted in Davis, Pohanka, and Troiani, *Civil War Journal,* p. 170.

50. Quoted in Davis, Pohanka, and Troiani, *Civil War Journal,* p. 170.

51. Quoted in Merrill, *Against Wind and Tide,* p. 241.

52. Quoted in Ward, *The Civil War,* p. 61.

53. Douglass, *Autobiographies,* pp. 791–92.

54. "Three Speeches from Frederick Douglass," taken from "Fighting Rebels with Only One Hand," *Douglass' Monthly,* September 1861. www.frederickdouglass.org/speeches/index.html.

55. Quoted in Noah Andre Trudeau, *Like Men of War.* Boston: Little, Brown, 1998, pp. 466–67.

56. "Three Speeches from Frederick Douglass," taken from "What the Black Man Wants," Annual Meeting of the Massachusetts Anti-Slavery Society, April 1865. www.frederickdouglass.org/speeches/index.html.

57. Quoted in Davis, Pohanka, and Troiani, *Civil War Journal,* p. 161.

Chapter 3: Commanders of the Confederacy

58. Quoted in Davis, Pohanka, and Troiani, *Civil War Journal*, p. 138.
59. Quoted in Davis, Pohanka, and Troiani, *Civil War Journal*, p. 142.
60. Quoted in Ward, *The Civil War*, p. 139.
61. Quoted in Davis, Pohanka, and Troiani, *Civil War Journal*, p. 148.
62. Quoted in Davis, Pohanka, and Troiani, *Civil War Journal*, p. 151.
63. Robert E. Lee, *The War Time Papers of R. E. Lee*. Boston: Little, Brown, 1961, pp. 692–93.
64. Lee, *The War Time Papers of R. E. Lee*, p. 722.
65. Quoted in Gregory Jaynes, *The Killing Ground: Wilderness to Cold Harbor*. Alexandria, VA: Time-Life Books, 1986, p. 156.
66. Quoted in Ward, *The Civil War*, p. 294.
67. Lee, *The War Time Papers of R. E. Lee*, p. 848.
68. Quoted in Foote, *The Civil War*, vol. 3, p. 941.
69. Quoted in Foote, *The Civil War*, vol. 3, p. 951.
70. Quoted in Davis, Pohanka, and Troiani, *Civil War Journal*, p. 159.
71. Quoted in Emory M. Thomas, *Robert E. Lee*. New York: W. W. Norton, 1995, p. 413.
72. Byron Farwell, *Stonewall*. New York: W. W. Norton, 1992, p. 19.
73. Quoted in Farwell, *Stonewall*, p. 24.
74. Quoted in Farwell, *Stonewall*, p. 26.
75. Quoted in Farwell, *Stonewall*, p. 55.
76. Quoted in Farwell, *Stonewall*, p. 115.
77. Quoted in Davis, Pohanka, and Troiani, *Civil War Journal*, p. 87.
78. Quoted in Farwell, *Stonewall*, p. 96.
79. Quoted in William C. Davis, ed., *Great Battles of the Civil War*. New York: Gallery Books, 1984, p. 72.
80. Quoted in Davis, Pohanka, and Troiani, *Civil War Journal*, p. 96.
81. Quoted in Farwell, *Stonewall*, p. 393.
82. Quoted in Ward, *The Civil War*, p. 211.
83. Quoted in Farwell, *Stonewall*, p. 528.
84. Lee, *The War Time Papers of R. E. Lee*, p. 484.

Chapter 4: Commanders of the Union

85. Quoted in Davis, Pohanka, and Troiani, *Civil War Journal*, p. 189.
86. Quoted in Davis, Pohanka, and Troiani, *Civil War Journal*, p. 192.
87. Ulysses S. Grant, *Memoirs and Selected Letters of U. S. Grant*. New York: Library of America, 1990, pp. 164–65.
88. Quoted in Ward, *The Civil War*, pp. 120–21.
89. Quoted in Ward, *The Civil War*, p. 281.
90. Quoted in A. A. Hoehling, *Vicksburg: 47 Days of Siege*. Englewood Cliffs, NJ: Prentice-Hall, 1969, p. 279.
91. Quoted in William S. McFeely, *Grant*. New York: W. W. Norton, 1981, p. 159.
92. Quoted in Ward, *The Civil War*, p. 280.
93. Quoted in Ward, *The Civil War*, p. 281.
94. Quoted in Ward, *The Civil War*, p. 258.
95. Quoted in T. Harry Williams, *McClellan, Sherman, and Grant*. New Brunswick, NJ: Rutgers University Press, 1962, p. 107.

96. Quoted in Davis, Pohanka, and Troiani, *Civil War Journal,* p. 198.

97. Quoted in Ward, *The Civil War,* p. 309.

98. Quoted in Foote, *The Civil War,* vol. 3, p. 939.

99. Quoted in Foote, *The Civil War,* vol. 3, p. 949.

100. Quoted in Foote, *The Civil War,* vol. 3, p. 947.

101. Quoted in Davis, Pohanka, and Troiani, *Civil War Journal,* p. 201.

102. Quoted in Ward, *The Civil War,* p. 411.

103. Quoted in Davis, Pohanka, and Troiani, *Civil War Journal,* pp. 205–206.

104. Quoted in B. H. Liddell Hart, *Sherman: Soldier, Realist, American.* New York: Dodd, Mead, 1929, p. 54.

105. Quoted in Burke Davis, *Sherman's March.* New York: Random House, 1980, p. 15.

106. Quoted in Ward, *The Civil War,* p. 74.

107. Quoted in Davis, *Sherman's March,* p. 130.

108. Quoted in Davis, Pohanka, and Troiani, *Civil War Journal,* p. 350.

109. Quoted in Foote, *The Civil War,* vol. 3, p. 318.

110. Quoted in Davis, *Sherman's March,* p. 31.

111. Quoted in Ward, *The Civil War,* p. 323.

112. Quoted in Foote, *The Civil War,* vol. 3, p. 491.

113. Quoted in Foote, *The Civil War,* vol. 3, p. 530.

114. Quoted in Ward, *The Civil War,* p. 331.

115. Quoted in Davis, Pohanka, and Troiani, *Civil War Journal,* p. 355.

116. Quoted in Foote, *The Civil War,* vol. 3, p. 651.

117. Quoted in Foote, *The Civil War,* vol. 3, p. 645.

118. Quoted in Foote, *The Civil War,* vol. 3, p. 794.

119. Quoted in Foote, *The Civil War,* vol. 3, p. 835.

120. Quoted in Davis, *Sherman's March,* p. 294.

121. William Tecumseh Sherman, *The Memoirs of General W. T. Sherman.* New York: Library of America, 1990, p. 870.

122. Quoted in Davis, *Sherman's March,* p. 298.

123. Quoted in Hart, *Sherman,* p. 425.

Chapter 5: The Cavalrymen

124. Quoted in Emory M. Thomas, *Bold Dragoon.* New York: Harper and Row, 1986, p. 61.

125. Quoted in Davis, Pohanka, and Troiani, *Civil War Journal,* p. 280.

126. Quoted in Thomas, *Bold Dragoon,* p. 128.

127. Thomas, *Bold Dragoon,* p. 147.

128. Quoted in Davis, Pohanka, and Troiani, *Civil War Journal,* p. 288.

129. Quoted in Davis, Pohanka, and Troiani, *Civil War Journal,* p. 333.

130. Quoted in Thomas, *Bold Dragoon,* p. 246.

131. Quoted in Thomas, *Bold Dragoon,* p. 252.

132. Quoted in Thomas, *Bold Dragoon,* p. 292.

133. Quoted in Thomas, *Bold Dragoon,* p. 293.

134. Quoted in Thomas, *Bold Dragoon,* p. 293.

135. Quoted in Davis, Pohanka, and Troiani, *Civil War Journal,* p. 299.

136. Quoted in Brian Steel Wills, *A Battle from the Start: The Life of Nathan Bedford Forrest.* New York: HarperCollins, 1992, p. 12.

137. Quoted in Wills, *A Battle from the Start,* p. 71.

138. Quoted in Wills, *A Battle from the Start,* p. 56.

139. Quoted in Ward, *The Civil War,* p. 271.

140. Quoted in Wills, *A Battle from the Start,* p. 64.

141. Bruce Catton, *Never Call Retreat.* Garden City, NY: Doubleday, 1965, p. 33.

142. Quoted in Ward, *The Civil War,* p. 346.

143. Quoted in Wills, *A Battle from the Start,* p. 139.

144. Quoted in Wills, *A Battle from the Start,* p. 145.

145. Quoted in Foote, *The Civil War,* vol. 3, p. 112.

146. Quoted in Wills, *A Battle from the Start,* p. 1.

147. Quoted in Wills, *A Battle from the Start,* p. 217.

148. Quoted in Wills, *A Battle from the Start,* p. 317.

149. Quoted in Wills, *A Battle from the Start,* p. 359.

150. Quoted in Wills, *A Battle from the Start,* p. 378.

151. Quoted in Wills, *A Battle from the Start,* p. 381.

152. Quoted in Roy Morris Jr., *Sheridan.* New York: Crown, 1992, p. 14.

153. Quoted in Morris, *Sheridan,* p. 41.

154. Quoted in Clarence Edward Macartney, *Grant and His Generals.* New York: McBride, 1953, p. 114.

155. Quoted in Ward, *The Civil War,* p. 261.

156. Quoted in Davis, Pohanka, and Troiani, *Civil War Journal,* p. 343.

157. Quoted in Morris, *Sheridan,* p. 164.

158. Quoted in Thomas, *Bold Dragoon,* p. 288.

159. Quoted in Davis, Pohanka, and Troiani, *Civil War Journal,* p. 340.

160. Quoted in Foote, *The Civil War,* vol. 3, p. 564.

161. Quoted in Morris, *Sheridan,* p. 179.

162. Quoted in Davis, Pohanka, and Troiani, *Civil War Journal,* p. 342.

163. Quoted in Foote, *The Civil War,* vol. 3, p. 919.

164. Quoted in Morris, *Sheridan,* p. 256.

Chapter 6: Women of Courage

165. Elizabeth D. Leonard, *Yankee Women: Gender Battles in the Civil War.* New York: W. W. Norton, 1994, p. 198.

166. Quoted in Elizabeth Brown Pryor, *Clara Barton: Professional Angel.* Philadelphia: University of Pennsylvania Press, 1987, p. 19.

167. Quoted in Pryor, *Clara Barton,* p. 21.

168. Quoted in Pryor, *Clara Barton,* p. 61.

169. Quoted in Pryor, *Clara Barton*, p. 84.
170. Quoted in Pryor, *Clara Barton*, p. 89.
171. Quoted in Pryor, *Clara Barton*, p. 93.
172. Quoted in Pryor, *Clara Barton*, p. 99.
173. Quoted in Pryor, *Clara Barton*, pp. 102, 124–25.
174. Quoted in Pryor, *Clara Barton*, p. 126.
175. Quoted in Pryor, *Clara Barton*, p. 129.
176. Quoted in Pryor, *Clara Barton*, p. 136.
177. Quoted in Pryor, *Clara Barton*, p. 346.
178. Quoted in Ward, *The Civil War*, p. 146.
179. Quoted in Leonard, *Yankee Women*, p. 109.
180. Quoted in Leonard, *Yankee Women*, p. 116.
181. Quoted in Leonard, *Yankee Women*, p. 123.
182. Quoted in Leonard, *Yankee Women*, p. 128.
183. Quoted in Leonard, *Yankee Women*, p. 128.
184. Quoted in Leonard, *Yankee Women*, p. 130.
185. Quoted in Leonard, *Yankee Women*, p. 136.
186. Quoted in Leonard, *Yankee Women*, pp. 138–39.
187. Quoted in Leonard, *Yankee Women*, p. 151.
188. Leonard, *Yankee Women*, p. 200.

Chapter 7: Out of Many, One

189. Sherman, *The Memoirs of General W. T. Sherman*, p. 870.
190. Quoted in Ward, *The Civil War*, p. 273.
191. Quoted in Merrill, *Against Wind and Tide*, p. 331.
192. Bruce Catton, *Reflections on the Civil War*. Garden City, NY: Doubleday, 1981, p. 226.
193. Quoted in Foote, *The Civil War*, vol. 3, p. 813.

★ For Further Reading ★

Doris Faber, *I Will Be Heard*. New York: Lothrop, Lee & Shepard, 1970. Account of the life of abolitionist William Lloyd Garrison.

Albert Marrin, *Unconditional Surrender*. New York: Atheneum, 1994. Well-written biography of Ulysses S. Grant from his birth to his death from throat cancer in 1885.

————, *Virginia's General*. New York: Atheneum, 1994. Biography of Robert E. Lee, beloved leader of the Confederate army.

Milton Meltzer, ed., *Frederick Douglass: In His Own Words*. New York: Harcourt Brace, 1995. Excerpts from the great abolitionist and orator's autobiographies.

————, ed., *Lincoln: In His Own Words*. New York: Harcourt Brace, 1993. A collection of Abraham Lincoln's most famous and moving speeches, interspersed with material about the sixteenth president's life.

Robert R. Potter, *Jefferson Davis*. Austin, TX: Steck-Vaughn, 1994. Biography of the first president of the Confederacy.

James Reger, *Civil War Generals of the Confederacy*. San Diego: Lucent Books, 1999. Biographies of several prominent Confederate generals of the Civil War.

Rafael Tilton, *Clara Barton*. San Diego: Lucent Books, 1995. Thorough biography of Clara Barton, enhanced with many primary-source quotes from Barton's letters and diary.

Nancy Whitelaw, *Clara Barton: Civil War Nurse*. Springfield, NJ: Enslow, 1997. Life and accomplishments of the "Angel of the Battlefield" and founder of the American Red Cross.

Diane Yancey, *Civil War Generals of the Union*. San Diego: Lucent Books, 1999. Biographies of several prominent Union generals in the war, including Ulysses S. Grant, William T. Sherman, and Philip Sheridan.

✫ Works Consulted ✫

Books

Bruce Catton, *Never Call Retreat*. Garden City, NY: Doubleday, 1965. The third volume of Catton's Centennial History of the Civil War Series focusing on the latter half of the war; contains material on many notable military leaders.

———, *Reflections on the Civil War*. Garden City, NY: Doubleday, 1981. Discussion of various war topics ranging from army food to Abraham Lincoln, slavery to submarines.

———, *This Hallowed Ground*. Garden City, NY: Doubleday, 1956. Excellent overview of the Civil War from the North's perspective.

Burke Davis, *Sherman's March*. New York: Random House, 1980. Complete account of Sherman's march through Georgia and the Carolinas.

Jefferson Davis, *Rise and Fall of the Confederate Government*. 2 vols. New York: D. Appleton, 1881. Memoirs of the president of the Confederate States of America; several appendixes include the Confederate constitution, and correspondence and speeches made by Davis during his political career.

William C. Davis, *Jefferson Davis: The Man and His Hour*. New York: Harper-Collins, 1991. Well-written biography of the controversial president of the Confederate States of America.

William C. Davis ed., *Great Battles of the Civil War*. New York: Gallery Books, 1984. Comprehensive account of nineteen major battles of the war, documented with primary-source letters, newspaper articles, maps, and quotes.

William C. Davis, Brian C. Pohanka, and Don Troiani, eds., *Civil War Journal: The Leaders*. Nashville: Rutledge Hill Press, 1997. Compilation of biographies covering a number of leaders of the Civil War; includes well-knowns such as Lee and Grant as well as less familiar individuals such as Nathan Bedford Forrest.

Frederick Douglass, *Autobiographies*. New York: Library of America, 1994. Three complete autobiographies written by former slave and abolitionist Frederick Douglass.

Byron Farwell, *Stonewall*. New York: W. W. Norton, 1992. Comprehensive biography of Confederate military legend Thomas "Stonewall" Jackson.

Shelby Foote, *The Civil War: A Narrative*. 3 vols. New York: Random House, 1958–1974. A three-volume work that provides a vivid, understandable overview of the people, battles, and issues of the Civil War.

Ulysses S. Grant, *Memoirs and Selected Letters of U. S. Grant.* New York: Library of America, 1990. The memoirs of one of the most enigmatic generals of the Civil War; deals with his life as a soldier and includes selected letters dating from 1839 to 1865.

B. H. Liddell Hart, *Sherman: Soldier, Realist, American.* New York: Dodd, Mead, 1929. In-depth study of the character and career of William Tecumseh Sherman.

Burton J. Hendrick, *Statesmen of the Lost Cause.* New York: Literary Guild of America, 1939. Portrayal of several Confederate statesmen, including Jefferson Davis, and their efforts to lead the South during the Civil War.

A. A. Hoehling, *Vicksburg: 47 Days of Siege.* Englewood Cliffs, NJ: Prentice-Hall, 1969. An account of the siege of Vicksburg through the eyes of some of its participants.

Gregory Jaynes, *The Killing Ground: Wilderness to Cold Harbor.* Alexandria, VA: Time-Life Books, 1986. Brief, well-illustrated overview of U. S. Grant's bloody campaign against R. E. Lee from the Battle of the Wilderness to the disaster at Cold Harbor.

Robert Underwood Johnson, ed., *Battles and Leaders of the Civil War.* Vol. 1. New York: Century, 1887. A compilation of articles on the Civil War, written primarily by participants in the conflict; includes contributions by Generals Ulysses Grant, Ambrose Burnside, Pierre G. T. Beauregard, Joseph E. Johnston, and others.

Robert E. Lee, *The War Time Papers of R. E. Lee.* Boston: Little, Brown, 1961. Includes Robert E. Lee's official correspondence—letters, orders, dispatches, and battle reports—plus letters to his family; provides a glimpse into the mind of one of the South's most beloved heroes.

Elizabeth D. Leonard, *Yankee Women: Gender Battles in the Civil War.* New York: W. W. Norton, 1994. Account of three women who challenged nineteenth-century biases to serve the Union during the Civil War.

Clarence Edward Macartney, *Grant and His Generals.* New York: McBride, 1953. Relationships between general in chief Ulysses S. Grant and the generals he commanded; includes chapters on Philip Sheridan, William T. Sherman, and others.

William S. McFeely, *Grant.* New York: W. W. Norton, 1981. Biography of one of the great military heroes of the war who was a failure in everything but marriage and battle.

Walter M. Merrill, *Against Wind and Tide.* Cambridge, MA: Harvard University Press, 1963. In-depth biography of abolitionist William Lloyd Garrison, with emphasis on Garrison's character as well as his antislavery endeavors.

Roy Morris Jr., *Sheridan.* New York: Crown, 1992. Biography of the fiery cavalry general who rose to fame in the Civil War.

Elizabeth Brown Pryor, *Clara Barton: Professional Angel*. Philadelphia: University of Pennsylvania Press, 1987. Portrait of the "Angel of the Battlefield," with emphasis on her character and personal life as well as her contributions during and after the Civil War.

William Tecumseh Sherman, *The Memoirs of General W. T. Sherman*. New York: Library of America, 1990. Vivid, firsthand account of the life of one of the most colorful Union generals of the war, including many of his wartime letters, orders, and reports.

Emory M. Thomas, *Bold Dragoon*. New York: Harper and Row, 1986. The life and achievements of flamboyant Confederate cavalryman J. E. B. Stuart.

———, *Robert E. Lee*. New York: W. W. Norton, 1995. A thorough examination of the life of the greatest Confederate military hero.

Noah Andre Trudeau, *Like Men of War*. Boston: Little, Brown, 1998. Complete history of black soldiers in the Civil War, beginning with the first unofficial ex-slave regiments organized in 1861.

Geoffrey C. Ward, *The Civil War: An Illustrated History*. New York: Knopf, 1990. Fascinating account of the Civil War with extensive period photos; companion volume to the PBS television documentary series *The Civil War* by Ken and Ric Burns.

T. Harry Williams, *McClellan, Sherman, and Grant*. New Brunswick, NJ: Rutgers University Press, 1962. Brief look at the careers of three Union generals and how their characters affected their leadership in the war.

Brian Steel Wills, *A Battle from the Start: The Life of Nathan Bedford Forrest*. New York: HarperCollins, 1992. Biography of the "Wizard of the Saddle," Confederate cavalryman Nathan Bedford Forrest.

Internet Sources

Boston African American National Historic Site Biographies, "William Lloyd Garrison." Taken from William S. Parsons and Margaret A. Drew, *The African Meeting House in Boston: A Sourcebook*. n.p., n.d. www.nps.gov/boaf/garris~1.htm.

The History Place, Great Speeches, "William Lloyd Garrison on the Death of John Brown," December 2, 1859. www.historyplace.com/speeches/garrison.htm.

"Three Speeches from Frederick Douglass." Taken from Philip S. Foner, *The Life and Writings of Frederick Douglass*. 5 vols. International Publishers, n.d. www.frederickdouglass.org/speeches/index.html.

Mary Edwards Walker, *Hit*. New York: American News Company, 1871. www.drake.edu/univannounce/dbhwebwork/hit.html.

★ Index ★

★ Picture Credits ★

Cover photo: Digital Stock

Corbis, 7, 8, 18, 78, 86, 100

Corbis-Bettmann, 20, 26, 29, 30, 37, 38, 42, 53, 64, 65, 66, 67, 70, 71, 83, 102, 105

Corbis/Minnesota Historical Society, 90

Digital Stock, 5, 13, 27, 33, 35, 40, 46, 48, 51, 58, 59, 75, 88, 93, 95, 96, 97, 110, 111

Dover Publications, Incorporated, 16

Library of Congress, 11, 23, 43, 44, 56, 61, 74, 79, 107

National Archives, 104

North Wind Picture Archives, 81

★ About the Author ★

Like many Americans, Diane Yancey finds the Civil War one of the most fascinating and romantic periods of U.S. history. She is the author of *Civil War Generals of the Union* and *Strategic Battles.*

Along with her interest in writing and the Civil War, she likes to collect old books, travel, and enjoy life in the Pacific Northwest with her husband, two daughters, and two cats. Her other books include *Desperadoes and Dynamite, The Hunt for Hidden Killers, Camels for Uncle Sam, Life in a Japanese American Internment Camp,* and *Life in Charles Dickens's England.*